SUICIDE
AMONG
GIFTED CHILDREN
AND ADOLESCENTS

D1566559

SUICIDE
AMONG
GIFTED CHILDREN
AND ADOLESCENTS

UNDERSTANDING
THE SUICIDAL MIND

TRACY L. CROSS, PH.D.

PRUFROCK PRESS INC.
WACO, TEXAS

Acknowledgements

Several people helped in creating this book. I would like to thank Lori Andersen for her work, especially on compiling the resources. I would also like to thank Natalie Dudnytska for her assistance with the chapter summaries. I would like to thank Dr. Jennifer Cross for her editing work and ideas shared throughout the process. And I would like to thank Lacy Compton for her work editing this book. I thank Joel McIntosh for supporting this project, knowing that it would likely appeal to a relatively small readership.

Dedication

I would like to dedicate this book to Ben and his family—Roger, Sherry, and Amanda.

Library of Congress Cataloging-in-Publication Data

Cross, Tracy L.
Suicide among gifted children and adolescents : understanding the suicidal mind / by
Tracy L. Cross, Ph.D.
    pages cm
Includes bibliographical references.
ISBN 978-1-61821-050-0 (pbk.)
1. Gifted children. 2. Suicidal behavior. 3. Teenagers--Suicidal behavior. 4. Suicide--
Psychological aspects. I. Title.
BF723.G5.C767 2013
362.28083--dc23
                          2013000226

Prufrock Press Inc.
P.O. Box 8813
Waco, TX 76714-8813
Phone: (800) 998-2208
Fax: (800) 240-0333
http://www.prufrock.com

TABLE OF CONTENTS

FOREWORD

I am pleased to provide a few words regarding Tracy Cross's unique contribution, *Suicide Among Gifted Children and Adolescents*. This book provides necessary information regarding the prevalence of the act itself, the risk factors associated with it, and helpful ideas on how schools can attempt to modify or eliminate this scourge.

Dr. Cross points out that "Clearly suicide is commonplace, pervasive in our society, and preventable." Because there is a multitude of evidence presented in this volume to verify that statement, we might reflect on why it is so rarely a topic considered in our schools and journals. The myth that "suicide is a sudden event that occurs out of nowhere and is unpredictable" maintains itself despite its falsity. Can it be that such a belief relieves all of us of responsibility to take action on this devastating problem? We are fortunate that Dr. Cross has collected this impressive data that calls on all of us to pay attention and act.

One of the useful discoveries from the data is the age most at risk. Adolescence appears to be the most vulnerable age, much more so than later college-age students. Apparently, many adolescents have not been able to develop positive coping skills to deal with the depression and social problems often attendant to that age and conclude from their hopelessness that ending things is the only answer.

The greater prevalence of suicide in states with higher rates of gun ownership is an interesting fact. Apparently, access to a reliable tool may be the final factor in the recipe, because guns are much more reliable than poisons or knives to the person who has decided to act upon his or her despair.

The fact that suicide is no more prevalent among students with gifts and talents than among students with average abilities should not be seen as reassuring. In practically all other dimensions, being "gifted" is associated with positive factors such as greater health, friendships, etc. When such children prove just as vulnerable, that is proof again that it is personal ideation rather than reality that we are dealing with. Such children are as prone to depression and social isolation as other students.

In addition to the inevitable depression and despair among family and friends, we have a sense of loss of their special gifts: the sonata never written, the scientific cure never discovered, the political accomplishments never realized, the brilliant poetry never created. We can ill afford such loss of potential talent.

Cross's recommendation for schools are well advised. Both formal and informal screening of students should take place to identify early students at risk and to take positive action. Substitute behaviors can be encouraged, and positive behavior supports can be applied. A mental health committee to develop positive plans for individuals may operate similar to the Individualized Education Programs (IEPs) already in force and could be very helpful.

Also, the final section on national and state resources provides a good reference base for those looking for often-hard-to-find sources of information on this topic.

Dr. Cross has done his field, and all those who work in it, a valuable service in producing this volume. I believe it will be a much-quoted source for many years.

James J. Gallagher
University of North Carolina

PREFACE

Although I have been somewhat aware of suicide since childhood, I have not been preoccupied with it or even particularly focused on it. I suspect that my longstanding interest in music and art have kept me close to people in two arenas wherein suicidal behavior has higher prevalence rates than average (Ludwig, 1995). I have also had numerous friends and acquaintances from the LBGTQ community; another group at higher than average risk for suicidal behavior. The single thread across my life is that I grew up surrounded by gifted and talented people. As I matured, I worried about some of my friends and acquaintances as, occasionally, one would engage in suicidal ideation or make a suicide attempt. These experiences set the stage for my midcareer focus on the suicidal behavior of students with gifts and talents.

In April of 1994, while I was watching MTV News, I learned of the suicide of the alternative band Nirvana's singer/songwriter Kurt Cobain. I realized that we had lost an important musician and leader of disenfranchised youth. I feared that there would likely be a pronounced effect on the Cobain followers. For several months prior to Cobain's death, I had been involved in a yearlong evaluation of a residential high school for intellectually gifted students (Academy). Within a couple of weeks of Cobain's death, I was contacted by the dean of the college of education that administered the Academy and was apprised that it was prom night and that there had been a suicide within the school's student body. I also learned that the suicide had occurred one block away from the Academy's campus. I met the dean at the Academy to help, prior to his informing the students what had happened. The dean had the very difficult responsibility of telling the students, during their prom, about the suicide of one of their student body leaders.

I learned that same evening that a former student of the same school had killed himself a few months before while in a mental health institution. This student had been sent home from the school following a brief period of attendance, after a series of inappropriate behaviors were documented. The student spent a month in a mental health facility, came home for one day, was returned to the mental health facility, and later hanged himself in the facility. The school learned after his death that he had a long history of mental health problems and had made several attempts to kill himself before he attended the Academy. None of this information was shared with the Academy until after his death.

A task force was created by the dean to: (a) conduct a postvention, (b) prevent another suicide, and, (c) study the suicides at the school. A postvention is a plan to enter an environment after a tragedy or crisis and help ease the pain of those in the environment. Services were provided to students, families, and some faculty and staff after determining the extent to which individual community members were at risk. Postventions also attempt to prevent suicide contagion from occurring. To those ends, all students who were designated as at risk were attended to personally and over time. During the following summer months, a third student associated with the school killed himself at his original home high school. His suicidal journal entry is included at the front of the first chapter of this book. He was the third student who had attended the Academy for some period of time who had died by his own hand. In the ensuing 19 years, no additional suicides have occurred among students attending the Academy.

These three suicides required intensive, long-term study to understand. Three psychological autopsies were conducted, culminating in a special issue of the *Journal of Secondary Gifted Education* in 1996. Considerable study of the school environment was also undertaken before, during, and after the postvention. Eighteen months after the third suicide occurred, the dean asked me to take over the Academy as its Executive Director. Several policies had been changed as a function of the task force recommendations, including hiring a full-time clinical psychologist to work in the school. I was asked to stay as Executive Director of the school for a semester to try to calm the employees of the school, as the university's board of trustees was scheduled to vote on whether to shut the school down. Their concerns included both the suicides and a high level of acrimony that existed between the faculty and the Academy's administration. I ended up staying at the Academy for approximately 9 years with my primary objective being the students' mental well-being.

CONFLUENCE OF EVENTS

I was trained as an educational psychologist and a school psychologist with a background in counseling and focus on adolescents and gifted students. Over time, my specialty became the psychology of students with gifts and talents. Most of my research over the past 30 years has been focused in this area. Topics such as social coping, lived experience, and stigma of giftedness established the foundation for my shift to studying suicidal behavior. During this 30-year period, I have run programs and a residential high school for gifted students and founded the Center for Gifted Studies and Talent Development and the Institute for Research on the Psychology of Gifted Students at Ball State University (BSU). Currently, I serve as Executive Director of the Center for Gifted Education at The College of William and Mary, where I hold an endowed chair entitled The Jody and Layton Smith Professor of Psychology and Gifted Education. For 10 years prior to my stint at William and Mary, I served BSU as the George and Frances Ball Distinguished Professor of Psychology and Gifted Studies.

Since beginning the psychological autopsies in 1994, I have focused much of my research on the suicidal behavior of students who are gifted and talented. I have written numerous articles and book chapters and made a multitude of presentations, all leading up to this book. This book is intended to provide an easy-to-read compilation of research that applies to the suicidal behavior of school-aged children and adolescents. More specifically, the book emphasizes the school as the context for observing students with gifts and talents. It is the single location that brings together teachers, counselors, and parents with the potential for monitoring and preventing suicide. Schools provide windows into the lives of students in ways that do not exist otherwise. For example, students develop patterns of behavior that foretell problems. Friendships, frustrations, relationships, alcohol and/or drug use, and academic achievement can all be monitored and interventions can be put in place before these lead to the death of a student.

An important second reason for placing the school at the center of this work is because it allows for the three groups of adults (teacher, counselors, and parents), and others as need be, to collaborate for the best interest of the child. Parents have a good sense of their children, and often overhear things said by their children's friends. Teachers see changes in achievement and friendships and examples of bullying. Counselors often get brought in when there is a problem, (although for some gifted students, teachers and counselors become their friends). Counselors also have training about social and emotional development that is quite valuable, plus many of the predictable issues of students who are gifted are on topics about which the counselors are knowledgeable. Combined, this group makes for a powerful and informed force working to prevent suicide among students with gifts and talents. It is my hope that the book might help us prevent suicide among this population and any other children with whom we have contact.

CHAPTER 1

INTRODUCTION

I am having trouble deciding were to kill myself. I can
either do it here (home)
when no one is home
call the police before so they can clean up so my family
won't have to discover me
There is a chance the police would get there too soon and
save me
My family would probably have very bad memories if they
knew I did it in one of our trees
I can do it somewhere else someone would find me, call
the police, my family would never see me
This would receive more publicity, which would be shitty
for my parents and friends
Even though both are flawed I believe doing it somewhere
else is the best option.

The preceding statements were the last journal entry of an
intellectually gifted adolescent who completed suicide. It is presented as it was found relative to spacing, spelling, and overall
appearance. A few days after writing the entry, the 16-year-old
hanged himself in the rafters of the bus stop in front of his local
high school. This was the first piece of information that I obtained
upon taking on the psychological autopsy of this gifted student.

The death of a child is a parent's worst nightmare. It represents
many of the fears and doubts that raising children today elicit.
Many people in society believe that being gifted makes one more
vulnerable to suicide. Others believe the opposite—that giftedness
provides protection from suicidal behavior. In either case, when a
child dies by his or her own hand, nothing creates greater suffering

and sense of loss, and nothing is a greater tragedy for society. This book explores the phenomenon of suicide among students with gifts and talents. It attempts to provide the reader a coherent picture of what suicidal behavior is and will clarify what is known and what is unknown about the phenomenon. The book will introduce two major theories of suicide with compelling explanatory power. I describe some future research that is needed. Information that illustrates the lived experience of gifted students is provided that sets the stage for an emerging model of the suicidal behavior of this population. This theory sheds light on the suicidal mind of students with gifts and talents. From both traditional suicidal recommendations and the research specific to those who are gifted, I provide information on healing the suicidal mind and what we can do to prevent suicides among these students. The book ends with considerable resources available to help.

To that end, the book is divided into relatively brief chapters that are based on empirical research, direct observation, literature review, other researchers' findings and arguments, and a theory emerging from years of study. The book represents the level of understanding possible at this time in history. The primary motivation to write this book is to help keep our students alive. With that in mind, information about suicide, description of the lives of students with gifts and talents, and information about preventing suicide is provided. Within this rather somber topic is some relatively good news, however—found in Chapter 2 when comparisons of suicide ideation among groups are provided.

In addition to raising the consciousness of adults interested in this topic, I will offer a carefully drafted narrative that stays as close to the research base as possible. From this, I hope that a greater awareness of the suicidal behavior of students with gifts and talents will be had and that additional efforts to prevent suicides will be put in place. I also hope that additional research on the topic will be conducted.

WHAT IS SUICIDE?

To begin, it makes sense to define suicide. Suicide is often defined as the ending of one's own life. It is an intentional act. As simple and direct as it sounds, it has engendered considerable study during the 20th and 21st centuries. Suicide has been acknowledged and written about for thousands of years and its meanings vary greatly based on the cultural context in which it occurs. Durkheim (1951) claimed that "There are two sorts of extra-social causes to which one may, *a priori*, attribute an influence on the suicide rate: they are organic-psychic dispositions and the nature of the physical environment" (p. 57). From committing *hara kiri* as an act of taking responsibility for failure, embarrassment, or shame, to dying to avoid responsibility, to dying as a culmination of myriad psychological factors, the context and historical zeitgeist in which suicide occurs matters. This book concentrates on ending one's life in Western society, particularly in the United States. It emphasizes the phenomenon in the second half of the 20th and the first 12 years of the 21st centuries.

SUICIDAL BEHAVIOR

If I throw myself off Lookout Mountain
No more pain my soul to bare
No more worries about paying taxes
What to eat, what to wear
Who will end up with my records?
Who will end up with my tapes?
Who will pay my credit card bills?
Who's gonna pay for my mistakes?

— *"Lookout Mountain" by the Drive-By Truckers*

A more comprehensive conception of suicide is actually called *suicidal behavior* and includes four behaviors: ideation, gestures, attempts, and completions. Like the song lyrics above reveal, suicide

3

ideation is thinking about suicide. Considerable study has focused on suicide ideation, as it is widely believed by suicidologists to exist in virtually all completed suicides. Suicidal gestures are considered behaviors that are not meant to actually kill the person, but appear like they might. For example, a physically large intellectually gifted male at the Academy took nine aspirin. The event had a reason, but immediate death was not the desired outcome. Suicide attempts are just that, efforts to die that fail. Completed suicides are defined as killing oneself intentionally. In this book, I use the term *completed* in lieu of *committed* when describing suicide. This linguistic change is important, as it reflects the fact that suicides are associated with mental health issues, not legal matters, as it has been considered to be for many years. Moreover, those who work with families of people who have taken their own lives stress the importance to destigmatize suicide and the descriptor "completed" is both more appropriate and helpful in reducing stigmatization (B. Ball, personal communication, 1992). Figure 1 illustrates the relationship among these four suicidal behaviors.

One of the important ideas being conveyed by this simple figure is that virtually all suicides occur after a person has engaged in suicide ideation. It becomes the background that sets the stage for the gestures, attempts, and completions. Secondly, many, many more people think about suicide than gesture, attempt, and complete combined. The gesturing image is in dashes to represent the fact that it is the least understood and, in some ways, most difficult to document of the four behaviors. The actual proportion of gestures could be larger than the attempts category. We believe that there are many more gestures than completions, but it is not clear about the relationship to attempts. Finally, there are many times more the numbers of attempts compared to the number of completions. This completion ratio plays out somewhat differently based upon ethnicity and gender and access to lethal means to harm one's self. This book focuses on the suicide ideation and completions among students with gifts and talents. To get to that, however, basic information about suicide in general must set the stage.

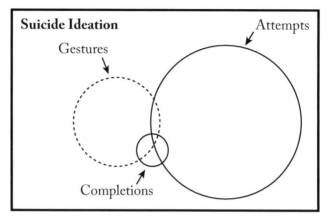

**The Relationship of
Suicidal Behaviors**

Suicide Ideation

Gestures

Attempts

Completions

Figure 1. The relationship of suicidal behaviors.

KEY POINTS FOR CHAPTER 1

❖ This book will discuss the phenomenon of suicide in the modern Western society, two major theories of suicide, recommendations on healing the suicidal mind, available resources, and suggestions for future research.

❖ Suicide is an intentional act of ending one's own life.

❖ The relationship of four suicidal behaviors—ideation, gestures, attempts, and completions—was discussed.

○ Ideation—thinking about suicide

○ Gestures—behaviors that are not meant to actually kill the person, but appear like they might

○ Attempts—efforts to die that fail

○ Completions—killing oneself intentionally

CHAPTER 2

BRIEF HISTORY
OF COMPLETED
SUICIDES

To understand suicidal behavior, specialists study prevalence rates. To that end, suicidologists rely on an equation: the number of people who complete suicide per 100,000 people per age group (X # per 100,000). For example, Table 1 below reveals that for all age groups in 2009 there was an average prevalence rate of 12.0 per 100,000 people. Given that rates are established in age bands (i.e., 5–14, 15–24, 25–34, 35–44, 45–54, 55–64, 65–74, 75–84), analyzing the particular prevalence rate by age can be considered historically and comparatively. We can consider the range in prevalence rates over time and as compared to the other age bands. We can consider historic effects and emerging patterns. All of these comparisons can be made, but only for completed suicides, far less so for the other three suicidal behaviors (ideation, gestures, attempts).

Comparisons can also be made geographically (see Tables 2 and 3). The analysis of suicide rate by census region shows that the prevalence rate of all age groups combined in the Northeast (9.8%) is well below the national average while the prevalence rate in the West (13.9%) is considerably higher. Of the 10 states with the highest prevalence rates, 9 are Western states, with the highest rates occurring in Wyoming, Alaska, Montana, Nevada, and New Mexico. The fewest absolute total numbers of suicides occurred in Vermont, North Dakota, and Delaware (each had 106), while California had the greatest number (3,913).

Table 1
Rates of Suicide in the United States per 100,000 People

Year	Ages 5–14	Ages 15–24	Ages 75–84	All ages
1999	0.6	10.1	18.1	10.5
2000	0.7	10.2	17.6	10.4
2001	0.7	9.9	17.4	10.7
2002	0.6	9.8	17.7	11.0
2003	0.6	9.6	16.4	10.9
2004	0.7	10.3	16.3	11.1
2005	0.7	9.9	16.8	11.0
2006	0.5	9.8	15.8	11.2
2007	0.5	9.6	16.2	11.5
2008	0.5	9.9	16.1	11.8
2009	0.6	10.0	15.8	12.0
2010	0.7	10.5	15.7	12.4

Note. Data compiled from Hoyert and Xu (2012).

Table 2
Suicide Rate by Region (2010)

Region	Rate per 100,000
Midwest	12.5
Northeast	9.8
South	12.8
West	13.9
Overall	12.4

Note. Data compiled from Hoyert and Xu (2012).

Table 3
Suicide Rate by State (2010)

Rank	State	Number	Rate Per 100.00
1	Wyoming	131	23.2
2	Alaska	164	23.1
3	Montana	227	22.9
4	Nevada	547	20.3
5	New Mexico	413	20.1
6	Idaho	290	18.5
7	Oregon	685	17.9
8	Colorado	865	17.2
9	South Dakota	140	17.2
10	Utah	473	17.1
11	Arizona	1,093	17.1
12	Vermont	106	16.9
13	Oklahoma	618	16.5
14	North Dakota	106	15.8
15	Arkansas	447	15.3
16	Hawaii	207	15.2
18	New Hampshire	196	14.9
19	Tennessee	943	14.9
20	Florida	2,789	14.8
21	Kentucky	631	14.5
22	Missouri	856	14.3
23	Washington	957	14.2
24	Alabama	679	14.2
25	Kansas	401	14.1
26	Maine	186	14.0
27	Wisconsin	793	13.9
28	South Carolina	637	13.8
29	Indiana	864	13.3

Table 3, *continued*

Rank	State	Number	Rate Per 100.00
30	Mississippi	388	13.1
31	Michigan	1,263	12.8
32	Ohio	1,439	12.5
33	Pennsylvania	1,576	12.4
34	North Carolina	1,174	12.3
35	Louisiana	557	12.3
36	Rhode Island	129	12.3
37	Iowa	372	12.2
38	Virginia	963	12.0
39	Delaware	106	11.8
40	Georgia	1,133	11.7
41	Texas	2,891	11.5
42	Minnesota	606	11.4
43	Nebraska	193	10.6
44	California	3,913	10.5
45	Connecticut	353	9.9
46	Illinois	1,178	9.2
47	Massachusetts	598	9.1
48	Maryland	502	8.7
49	New Jersey	719	8.2
50	New York	1,547	8.0
51	District of Columbia	41	6.8
	Overall	38,634	12.4

Note. Data compiled from Hoyert and Xu (2012).

In considering these varied rates by state, I speculated that states with the highest percentage of gun ownership might correspond with the highest rankings of completed suicide. The logic is that access to lethal means is an important correlate of suicide. In fact, this hypothesis has some support in the rates of gun ownership. A study of firearms ownership conducted by the North Carolina State Center for Health Statistics (2002; see http://www.schs.state.nc.us/SCHS/brfss/2001/us/firearm3.html) can be used to give context to this argument. The states highest in suicide rate also have high rates of gun ownership—Wyoming (23.2; 59.7%), Alaska (23.1; 57.8%), Montana (22.9; 57.7%), Nevada (20.3; 33.8%), and New Mexico (20.1; 34.8%); while the states lowest in suicide rate also have low rates of gun ownership—New York (8.0; 18%), New Jersey (8.2; 12.3%), Maryland (8.7; 21.3%), Massachusetts (9.1; 12.6%), and Illinois (9.2; 20.2%).

The following data are taken from National Vital Statistics Reports and the CDC WISQARS data reporting system (Hoyert & Xu, 2012; see http://www.cdc.gov/nchs/products/nvsr.htm). This information helps us to visualize and understand patterns of suicidal behavior in the US.

❖ 1.5% of all deaths are from suicide.

❖ On average, one suicide occurs every 14 minutes.

❖ Suicide is the 10th leading cause of death for all Americans.

❖ Suicide is the third leading cause of death for young people aged 15–24.

❖ Suicide is the fourth leading cause of death for 25–44 year olds.

❖ Suicide is the leading cause of death among college students (Turner & Keller, 2011).

❖ Male suicides occur at nearly four times the rate of female suicides. In 2010, 30,277 males died by suicide while 8,087 females died by suicide.

❖ In the U.S., death by suicide occurs more than twice as frequently as death by homicide. In 2010, 38,364 completed suicide, while 16,259 were victims of homicide.

❖ There were approximately 1,000,000 reported suicide attempts in 2010.

Clearly suicide is commonplace, pervasive in our society, and preventable. Suicidologists are becoming increasingly more sophisticated about the phenomenon. However, preventing suicidal behavior is complicated and requires the expertise of myriad professionals. For example, policy makers, healthcare professionals, researchers, philosophers, educators, and others have great potential for helping fix this societal problem.

An examination of suicide rates over an extended time period allows trends to be studied (see Table 4 and Figure 2). Across time, the youngest group has had the lowest incidence rates, while the highest rates were in the oldest groups. The data show that adolescents were less likely to complete suicide than adults. However, the trends over time for these groups were very different. Since 1950, the overall suicide rate has decreased from 13.2 to 12.4. During this time span, youth (ages 5–24) suicide rates have more than doubled, while older adult (ages 55–85+) suicide rates have declined dramatically. The suicide rates for the 35–54 age group have remained relatively constant. In 1950, the suicide rates for older adults (26.8 to 31.1) were more than five times the rate for adolescents aged 15 to 24 (4.5). By 2010, the rates for older adults ranged from 13.7 to 17.6 while the rate for adolescents was 10.5. In 2010, the rate for older adults was less than twice the rate for adolescents. Thus, although the current rates for youth suicide may not appear to be disproportionate to the overall population rates, the trends observed over time for these groups are quite different.

Developmental differences and life differences between these age groups imply that the rationalizations these individuals use to justify suicidal behaviors are profoundly different. Youth suicidal behavior tends to be driven by the desire to escape relatively temporal emotional pains (Schneidman, 1993), while the need to be free of chronic physical pain is a common rationalization of suicidal behavior for the elderly. Young people have immature notions of permanence compared to older people, and this

Table 4
A 60-Year Look at Prevalence Rates

	All Ages	Ages 5–14	Ages 15–24	Ages 25–34	Ages 35–44	Ages 45–54	Ages 55–64	Ages 65–74	Ages 75–84	Ages 85+
1950	13.2	0.2	4.5	9.1	14.3	20.9	26.8	29.6	31.1	28.8
1960	13.2	0.3	5.2	10	14.2	20.7	23.7	23	27.9	26
1970	13.2	0.3	8.8	14.1	16.9	20	21.4	20.8	21.2	19
1980	13.2	0.4	12.3	16	15.4	15.9	15.9	16.9	19.1	19.2
1990	12.5	0.8	13.2	15.2	15.3	14.8	16	17.9	24.9	22.2
2000	10.4	0.7	10.2	12	14.5	14.4	12.1	12.5	17.6	19.6
2010	12.4	0.7	10.5	14	16	19.6	17.5	13.7	15.7	17.6

Note. Rates are per 100,000. Data compiled from Centers for Disease Control and Prevention (CDC, 2013).

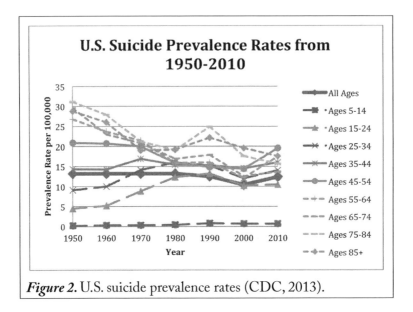

Figure 2. U.S. suicide prevalence rates (CDC, 2013).

becomes an essential factor in the suicide decision. Older people have a better sense of temporality because of their life experiences. Furthermore, the emotional pains of youth will subside, while the physical pains of the elderly often worsen. Therefore, suicide ideation is a qualitatively different phenomenon among diverse age groups.

COMMON METHODS OF COMPLETING SUICIDE

People have found myriad ways to kill themselves. Some of the popular methods from times past included poison, jumping from cliffs, and knives or swords. Contemporary approaches are wide ranging, from firearms to hanging. In some cases, such as car wrecks and suicide by cop (inducing police officers to shoot oneself), psychological autopsies must be performed to determine cause of death relative to intent. More on psychological autopsy will appear in Chapter 6.

In recent times, important differences have existed between males and females relative to suicide attempts, completions, and approaches taken. Firearms, suffocation, and poisons (including drugs/pharmaceuticals) are the most common methods of suicide. Tables 5 and 6 illustrate the differences.

Table 7 illustrates suicide-related behavior among students in grades 9–12 during the past 12 months prior to the survey being conducted. Table 8 reflects the suicide-related behavior for 10 years among both high school and college students. As illustrated in the table, rates reflecting those seriously considering suicide and those who have made an attempt have an overall declining trend. This is good news.

The grouping of students aged 15–24 into one category in National Vital Statistics Reports masks developmental differences among those who engage in suicidal behavior. The American College Health Association and the Centers for Disease Control Division of Adolescent and School Health each collect data that can be compared to see these developmental differences (CDC, 2013; see Table 8). The data show significantly lower rates of (a) seriously considering and (b) attempting suicide for college students compared to high school students. In 2011, high school students attempted suicide at a rate that was 10 times greater than the rate for college students, and seriously considered suicide at a rate that was more than three times higher than that for college students. Both groups showed a positive downward trend in suicidal behavior. The high school students represent a heterogeneous group while college students would be a more selective group relative to general ability, academic achievement, and life experience. Therefore, it seems that as students mature, they gain a better perspective on the temporality of emotionally painful situations.

Both age groups have seen declines in the rates of suicidal behaviors over the past decade, but the decrease was much larger for college students than for high school students. This data implies that high school students are at significantly higher risk for suicidal behaviors, particularly for suicide attempts, than college students. It may be that students find greater acceptance in the

Table 5
Suicide Methods Used in the U.S.

Method	Percent of Total (38,364 Suicides)	Number of Suicides
Firearms	50.5%	19,392
Hanging, strangulation, suffocation	24.7%	9,493
Poisons	17.2%	6,599
All other methods	7.6%	2,880

Note. Data compiled from CDC (2013).

Table 6
Suicide Methods by Gender

Method	Men—Percent of Total	Men—Number of Suicides (30,277 Total)	Women—Percent of Total	Women—Number of Suicides (8,087 Total)
Firearms	56.0%	16,962	30.0%	2,430
Hanging, strangulation, suffocation	25.1%	7,592	23.5%	1,901
Poisons	11.8%	3,573	37.4%	3,026
All other methods	7.1%	2,150	9.1%	730

Note. Data compiled from CDC (2013).

college environment than in the high school environment because they are able to find a peer group that readily accepts them as they are. For students who are nonmodal (e.g., high-ability students), or who possess characteristics that make them feel very different from most of their peers, finding this acceptance in high school can be difficult.

Table 7

Suicide-Related Behaviors of Students in Grades 9–12
in the U.S. in 2011

Behavior (During the Last 12 Months Before the Survey)	Prevalence Rate (%)
Seriously considered attempting suicide	15.8
Made a plan about how they would attempt suicide	12.8
Attempted suicide one or more times	7.8
Suicide attempt resulting in an injury, poisoning, or an overdose that had to be treated by a doctor or nurse	2.4

Note. Data compiled from CDC (2013).

Table 8

Trends in Suicide-Related Behaviors of High School
and College Students in the U.S.

	2001	2003	2005	2007	2009	2011
Percent of High School Students Who Seriously Considered Suicide in Past 12 Months	19.0	16.9	16.9	14.5	13.8	15.8
Percent of High School Students Who Attempted Suicide in Past 12 Months	8.8	8.5	8.4	6.9	6.3	7.8
Percent of Undergraduate College Students Who Seriously Considered Suicide in Past 12 Months	10.5	10.3	10.2	9.8	3.8	4.4
Percent of Undergraduate College Students Who Attempted Suicide in Past 12 Months	1.8	1.3	1.5	1.6	0.7	0.7

Note. Data compiled from CDC (2013).

KEY POINTS FOR CHAPTER 2

* Suicidologists study prevalence rates that are established in age bands to understand suicidal behavior and to consider them historically and comparatively.

* Analysis of suicide rates by census region: highest suicide rates in 2010 were recorded in the Western U.S., especially in California, and the lowest rates were recorded in the Northeast.

* Lethal means is an important correlate of suicide. Hence, the states with the highest percentage of gun ownership correspond with the highest rankings of completed suicide.

* Suicide is the leading cause of death among college students.

* Suicide is commonplace, pervasive to our society, and preventable.

* Policy makers, health care professionals, researchers, philosophers, educators, and others have great potential for helping prevent suicide.

* Examination of suicide prevalence rates from 1950–2010 showed that while overall suicide rate has decreased, youth (ages 5–24) rates have more than doubled.

* Suicide ideation is a qualitatively different phenomenon among diverse age groups.

* The most common contemporary approaches to completing suicide are firearms and hanging, strangulation, or suffocation.

* High school students are at significantly higher risk for suicidal behaviors than college students.

CHAPTER 3

EXPANDING THE EPIDEMIOLOGICAL LENS FROM PREVALENCE RATES TO CORRELATES

To understand the specific research on students with gifts and talents and suicide, we must first illustrate the current knowledge of suicide among the general population of children, adolescents, and young adults beyond mere prevalence rates. Considerable research has been conducted on trying to predict completed suicides. To that end, risk factors have been established. Risk factors are established statistically by correlating different traits, qualities, and behaviors with completed or attempted suicides. Initial studies of risk factors were designed somewhat atheoretically. Over time, theories of suicide have been studied and to varying degrees empirically validated, complementing the epidemiological data. Two especially important theories will be discussed in Chapter 4. They represent two different, but powerful theories for making sense out of suicidal behavior. They are psychache (Schneidman, 1993) and the suicide trajectory model (Stillion & McDowell, 1996). Building on these theories, later in the book I will offer my own theory for the suicidal mind and suicidal behavior among students with gifts and talents.

It is important to understand not only how many people of different categories are engaged in suicidal behavior, but also know what is associated (statistically speaking, correlated) with suicide.

These correlates are often touted as being risk factors. To that end, considerable research has been conducted trying to uncover these correlates. For example, Rudd et al. (2006) attempted to more fully distinguish between the risk factors and warning signs of suicide. He concluded that risk factors tend to be stable characteristics such as age, suicide attempts, and comorbidity, while warning signs are more transitory states such as psychache and hopelessness. Warning signs will be discussed more fully in later chapters.

RISK FACTORS FOR ADOLESCENT SUICIDE

Gould, Greenberg, Velting, and Shaffer (2003) conducted a review of a decade's worth of research on adolescent suicide and described the following as significant risk factors (Gould et al., provided the comments within the parentheses):

1. Psychiatric disorders such as depression and anxiety (This is referred to as comorbidity and is very strongly associated with attempts and completions.)
2. Substance abuse (This can vary in type, but alcohol and other popular depressants are the more common types.)
3. Cognitive and personality factors (hopelessness, coping skills, neuroticism)
4. Aggressive-impulsive behavior
5. Sexual orientation (homosexual, bisexual)
6. Friend or family member of someone with suicidal behavior
7. Parental psychopathology (depression, substance abuse)
8. Stressful life circumstances (interpersonal loss, legal/disciplinary)
9. Glamorization of suicide through media coverage
10. Access to lethal methods (firearms)

Because most of these are self-explanatory, I will only comment on three of them (5, 9, 10). I begin with 5: sexual orientation (homosexual, bisexual). The issue is not being homosexual or bisexual per se, but rather it is a person's lived experience of being homosexual or bisexual relative to his or her treatment in society. This is an important distinction that is often politicized. In time, more sophisticated research in this area will be conducted by expanding the category to include the now commonly used term LGBTQ (lesbian, gay, bisexual, transgendered, or queer).

Number 9 on the list of risk factors, glamorization of suicide through media coverage, is a relatively recent finding and seems to be true for the period just following the Kurt Cobain suicide. Considerable attention in the media was paid to this event. For weeks, MTV and other news outlets aired programs about the life, death, and music of Kurt Cobain. This suicide was one of the major news events of 1994, and given the growing competition among the increasing number of 24-hour news stations, the amount of coverage was quite substantial.

The third risk factor to be noted is number 10 on the list: access to lethal methods (firearms). Of all of the 10 risk factors, this one draws the most concern from those who believe that it might have an effect on gun ownership. The issue is not about second amendment rights to own a gun, but rather the fact that when a suicidal person has immediate access to lethal means of death, chances of a successful suicide increase.

Gould et al.'s (2003) research is important because it brings together many previously conducted studies. The 10 risk factors of suicide become an important tool to help us understand variables associated with suicidal behavior. Although not causal per se, in some cases the correlations are quite strong. For example, depression and anxiety are very common states in which people who engage in suicidal behavior find themselves. This fact provides guidance about how to intervene to prevent suicide. Unfortunately, however, other correlates such as sexual orientation or whether a family member has completed suicide are not correlates that can be changed. However, correlation is not causation; even with the inherent limitations of relying on correlates as risk factors, having them greatly benefits our understanding and potential to inter-

vene in positive ways to help prevent completed suicides. Note that suicide prevention will be discussed in Chapter 9.

The American Association of Suicidology (n.d.) offered the information I have compiled into Table 9 as an easy-to-remember consensus of warning signs of suicide.

Although not exactly the same as the previous list of factors associated with suicide offered by Gould et al., it overlaps considerably. It also uses language that is less technical, making it easier to read and share with others. It is important to note that millions of people live long lives with one or more risk factors from the list above. Moreover, trying to predict actual suicide attempts from knowledge of an individual's factors has not been very successful.

A wonderful visual illustrating both factors that make people vulnerable to, and protected from, completed suicides is included in Table 10 (White, 2012), a quick guide for adults who want to familiarize themselves with predisposing, contributing, precipitating, and protective factors by key content as broken down into the categories of individual, family, peer, school, and community. Table 10 also provides the reader with ways that people are naturally protected from engaging in suicidal behavior and some ways to provide the protectors. The big picture represents an optimistic and somewhat thorough overview of factors associated with suicidal behavior.

One can easily imagine a person grappling with some of the factors while benefitting from others. However, the degree of influence across the factors varies widely and is somewhat less scientific than previous lists of factors. However, once again, there is considerable overlap with other, more scientific lists. The gestalt of Table 10 is that it is more phenomenological than merely listing factors. Many of the terms and phrases on this list, such as humiliation, are powerful examples of human experience that can be quite motivating when combined with other factors, such as feeling trapped or hopeless. In essence, one can imagine a person being increasingly weighted down as the number of, and/or severity of, the suicidal factors impacts him or her. This description of a phenomenological-developmental model of suicidal behavior is

Table 9
Consensus Warning Signs of Suicide

A person at risk for suicidal behavior most often will exhibit warning signs such as:

Letter	Represents	Description
I	Ideation	Expressed or communicated ideation • Threatening to hurt or kill him- or herself, or talking of wanting to hurt or kill him- or herself • Looking for ways to kill him- or herself by seeking access to firearms, available pills, or other means • Talking or writing about death, dying, or suicide when these actions are out of the ordinary
S	Substance Abuse	Increased substance (alcohol or drug) use
P	Purposelessness	No reasons for living; no sense of purpose in life
A	Anxiety	Anxiety; agitation; unable to sleep or sleeping all the time
T	Trapped	Feeling trapped—like there's no way out
H	Hopelessness	Hopelessness
W	Withdrawal	Withdrawing from friends, family, and society
A	Anger	Rage, uncontrolled anger, seeking revenge
R	Recklessness	Acting reckless or engaging in risky activities, seemingly without thinking
M	Mood Changes	Dramatic mood changes

Note. From American Association of Suicidology (n.d.).

Table 10
Suicide Risk and Protective Factors

Key Content	Predisposing Factors	Contributing Factors	Precipitating Factors	Protective Factors
Individual	• Previous attempt • Depression/psychiatric disorder • Prolonged or unresolved grief	• Rigid cognitive style • Poor coping skills • Substance abuse • Sexual orientation issues • Impulsivity • Hypersensitivity	• Personal failure • Humiliation • Trauma • Developmental crisis	• Easy temperament • Creative problem solving • Personal autonomy • Self-mastery experience • Optimistic outlook • Sense of humor
Family	• Suicidal behavior or completed suicide • Violence or abuse • Psychiatric disorders • Early childhood loss or separation	• Substance abuse • Instability • Ongoing conflict	• Loss of significant family member • Death by suicide	• Warmth and belonging in family relationships • Adults model healthy adjustments • High and realistic expectations
Peers	• Social isolation and alienation	• Negative attitudes toward seeking adult help • Modeling maladaptive behaviors	• Teasing/cruelty • Interpersonal loss • Rejection • Death by suicide	• Social competence • Healthy peer modeling • Acceptance and support

Table 10, *continued*

Key Content	Predisposing Factors	Contributing Factors	Precipitating Factors	Protective Factors
School	• Long-standing history of negative school experiences • Lack of meaningful connection	• Disruption during transitional periods • Staff reluctant or uncertain how to help	• Failure • Expulsion • Disciplinary crisis	• Adults who believe in them • Parent involvement • Participation encouraged
Community	• "Legacy" of suicide • Marginalization • Political disempowerment	• Media portrayal of suicide • Access to firearms or lethal methods • Gatekeepers reluctant or uncertain how to help • Inaccessible resources • Economic deprivation	• Celebrity death by suicide • Conflict with law or incarceration	• Opportunities to participate • Hope for the future • Self-determination and solidarity • Available resources

Note. Adapted from *Preventing Youth Suicide: A Guide for Practitioners* by J. White, 2012. Copyright 2012 by British Columbia Ministry of Children and Family Development. Adapted with permission.

the image that I am moving the reader to, away from a conception that is more associative or based on a list of factors.

Table 10 includes risk and protective factors from several perspectives, including the community. This particular perspective is usually outside of the emphasis of any book that is more school focused. It is included in this book, however, because schools are often situated within communities. Communities are also where media portrayals of suicide events of myriad famous people such as Kurt Cobain occur. It also supports the earliest contention of the book—that to understand suicides, one must understand the context in which they occur.

KEY POINTS FOR CHAPTER 3

❖ Suicide risk factors have been defined in order to predict completed suicides by correlating traits, qualities, and behaviors with completed or attempted suicides.

❖ Two theories important for understanding suicidal behaviors are psychache (Schneidman, 1993) and the suicide trajectory model (Stillion & McDowell, 1996).

❖ Significant risk factors for adolescent suicide, as defined by Gould et al. (2003), include psychiatric disorders, substance abuse, and cognitive and personality factors.

❖ Sexual orientation becomes a risk factor depending upon the experience of a person or his or her treatment in society.

❖ A relatively recent risk factor is glamorization of suicide through media coverage (e.g., suicide of Kurt Cobain).

❖ The access to lethal methods (firearms) risk factor is important because it increases chances of a successful suicide.

❖ Knowledge of the 10 risk factors benefits our understanding and potential to intervene in positive ways to help prevent completed suicides.

❖ Table 9, featuring information offered by the American Association of Suicidology in 2007, is a comprehensive way to remember consensus of warning signs of suicide.

❖ The suicide risk and protective factors table (Table 10; White & Morris, 2010) provides a phenomenological-developmental model of suicidal behavior.

CHAPTER 4

SUICIDE TRAJECTORY MODEL AND PSYCHACHE

In my understanding of the various theories associated with suicide, I have come to prefer two: Stillion and McDowell's (1996) suicide trajectory model and Schneidman's (1993) psychache. These two models resonate with my professional experience of suicide and seem to provide considerable explanatory power about suicidal behavior.

SUICIDE TRAJECTORY MODEL

Stillion and McDowell (1996) developed a theory-based model of suicide called the suicide trajectory model (STM; see Table 11), which includes associated risk factors. The emphasis of the theory is to predict risk for suicidal behavior.

The STM groups correlates of suicide into four categories (biological, psychological, cognitive, and environmental) that provide considerable breadth. This makes conceptual understanding of the numerous predictors of suicide in a theoretical manner manageable. It provides a conception of suicide that offers professionals numerous handles upon which to grasp as they try to prevent deaths. Metaphorically, it provides a categorical system of potential weights that lead the potentially suicidal person in the direction of suicide. The theory attempts to tie together the categories of factors in a coherent manner. Stillion and McDowell (1996) stated:

Table 11

Suicide Trajectory Model Categories and Associated Risk Factors

Category	Risk Factors
Biological	Gender (male) Race (Native American, White) Genetic bases (parental psychopathy) Sexual orientation (homosexual, bisexual) Serotonin dysfunction
Psychological	Low self-esteem Depressed mood Feelings of hopelessness/helplessness Aggressive-impulsive tendencies Poor coping strategies Existential questions
Cognitive	Poor social problem solving Inflexible thinking Negative self-talk Rigidity of thought
Environmental	Familial dysfunction (impaired parent-child relationships) Social isolation Stressful life circumstances (interpersonal loss) Presence of lethal methods Exposure to suicide completers (friends/family)

As we move through life, we encounter situations and events that add their weight to each risk factor category. When the combined weight of these risk factors reaches the point where coping skills are threatened with collapse, suicidal ideation is born. Once present, suicidal ideation seems to feed upon itself. It may be exhibited in warning signs and may be intensified by trigger events. In the final analysis, however, when the suicide attempt is made, it occurs because of the contributions of the four risk categories. (p. 21)

The limitation to the STM, however, is that it is largely made up of correlations or variables associated with suicidal behavior with limited influence from within the person. This is where Schneidman's (1993) work picks up as he moves the conversation from descriptive epidemiology and prediction with some explanation, to a theory that has been empirically validated focusing on the subjective experiences of the suicidal person. I believe this to be the most important contribution to research on the suicidal mind.

PSYCHACHE

I never thought I'd die alone
I laughed the loudest who'd have known?
I trace the cord back to the wall
No wonder it was never plugged in at all
I took my time, I hurried up
The choice was mine, I didn't think enough
I'm too depressed to go on
You'll be sorry when I'm gone

    —"Adam's Song" by Blink 182

Edwin Schneidman was a clinical psychologist and arguably the father of suicidology and thantology (the study of death and the care of the dying) in the U.S. He died in 2009. He spent his career focused on suicide, authoring 20 books and numerous articles about suicide, including one wherein he focused on survivors of suicide—1998's *The Suicidal Mind*. This book provides considerable information about the lived experience of suicide attempters: one of the three died, the second lived for several months before dying of infections, and the third survived but was disfigured by the attempt. Schneidman began the American Association of Suicidology and the journal *Suicide and Life Threatening Behavior*. He also coined the term *psychological autopsy*.

Psychological autopsy, while often used to determine equivocal deaths, has become an invaluable approach to studying the life of a person who completed suicide. My colleagues and I employed this approach in our early research (Cross, Cook, & Dixon, 1996) and again later (Cross, Gust-Brey, & Ball, 2004). From his many years in the field working with clients, and from previous research, Schneidman's (1993) theory asserted that suicide attempts come from the desire on the part of the person to escape intolerable psychological pain. He called this pain psychache. This profound pain's etiology includes several potential pathways and factors. Ultimately, when the pain is unbearable, suicide becomes the path to escape from the pain.

Schneidman (1993) believed that suicide has four elements: (a) heightened inimicality (hostility), (b) exacerbation of perturbation, (c) increased constriction of intellectual focus, and (d) cessation. Schneidman (1981) described inimicality as "qualities within the individual that are unfriendly towards the self" (p. 222). Perturbation "reflects how 'shook up', ill at ease, or mentally upset the person is" (p. 223). Constriction reflects the suicidal person's dichotomous thinking and unwillingness to consider the effects of suicide on others. Cessation occurs due to the belief that ending one's life will end the unbearable pain (psychache).

Over the years, Schneidman and others grew increasingly interested in the role that hopelessness plays in suicidal behavior. A few others picked up on this idea. For example, a study by DeLisle and Holden (2009) revealed that psychache and hopelessness both contribute variance to the prediction of suicide. This suggests that each can be valuable to understanding and preventing suicide.

Rudd et al. (2006) attempted to distinguish between the risk factors and warning signs of suicide. He claimed that risk factors tend to be stable characteristics such as age, history of attempts, and psychiatric diagnosis. Risk factors are thought to be distally related to suicide. On the other hand, warning signs such as psychache and hopelessness are thought to be proximally associated with suicidal behavior and suggest potentially imminent risk. Distal risk factors are thought to be the initial causative factors in the original environment, while proximal causes are current causative factors (Rudd et al., 2006).

Combining prevalence rates, correlates, and risk factors with the STM, Schneidman's (1993) theory of psychache, and the very recent research on hopelessness paints an increasingly comprehensive picture of the nature of suicide among the general population of the U.S. Despite the increasingly sophisticated level of understanding, it has proven to be very difficult to accurately predict suicide attempts and completions.

My view is that the STM provides us the capacity to look for students in distress. Schneidman's concept of psychache, plus the recent research on hopelessness, provides us with a great basic roadmap of understanding some of the salient aspects of the lived experience of suicidal behavior. When all of the variables are taken together, strategies and techniques for preventing suicide in school can be put in place. This will be explored later in the book in Chapter 8. But first, research that pertains to students with gifts and talents will be provided.

KEY POINTS FOR CHAPTER 4

❖ Stillion and McDowell's (1996) theory-based suicide trajectory model includes associated risk factors that are grouped into four categories (biological, psychological, cognitive, and environmental).

❖ Edwin Schneidman's (1993) work on suicide moves from descriptive epidemiology and prediction to a theory that has been empirically validated focusing on the subjective experiences of the suicidal person.

❖ The importance of Edwin Schneidman's input into suicidology and thanatology was discussed.

❖ Schneidman's (1993) theory asserts that suicide attempts come from the desire on the part of the person to escape intolerable psychological pain.

❖ Four elements of suicide as defined by Schneidman (1993) are: (a) heightened inimicality (hostility), (b) exacerbation of perturbation, (c) increased constriction of intellectual focus, and (d) cessation.

❖ Rudd et al. (2006) attempted to distinguish between the risk factors (distally related to suicide) and warning signs (proximally associated with suicidal behavior) of suicide.

❖ Understanding the nature of suicide will help us to develop and use strategies and techniques for preventing suicide in schools.

CHAPTER 5

CURRENT RESEARCH ON SUICIDAL BEHAVIOR OF STUDENTS WITH GIFTS AND TALENTS

SUICIDE AMONG GIFTED ADOLESCENTS

This topic is so important that it has drawn considerable attention from professionals who work on behalf of students with gifts and talents. A great deal has been published claiming that either gifted students are more susceptible to suicidal behavior or they have qualities that naturally protect them from this behavior. Although reasonable logic exists on both sides of the argument, neither side has brought any data to back up their assertions. Therefore, those articles will generally not be included in this book.

As noted in Chapter 2, typically the first step in studying suicide among subgroups begins with establishing the total numbers and prevalence rates. Surprisingly in the year 2013, the actual numbers and prevalence rates of suicide among students with gifts and talents are unknown. This is due in part because of the lack of a consensus definition of a gifted population (Cross, 1996a, 1996b; Delisle, 1986). Without knowing exactly who they are, we cannot be accurate in our estimates of prevalence rates. In addition, the statistics kept about people who died via suicide does not note whether they were identified as gifted.

Making this determination even more difficult is the fact that due to our commitment to local control, school districts often have differing definitions of giftedness. Consequently, if a student with gifts and talents happens to die via suicide in a school district that does not use the same definition as his or her previous school, then that information has little chance of becoming known. Each of the examples noted above have nuances that make following giftedness as a demographic variable almost impossible. Even with profound impediments to knowing absolute numbers and prevalence rates, like their nongifted peers, it is quite likely that gifted students are completing suicide and the incidence of suicidal behavior among both groups has followed the basic pattern wherein rates have recently decreased somewhat after many years of increase (Cross, 1996a, 1996b). Consequently, it is judicious to assume that the rates of suicidal behavior of gifted and nongifted same-aged students are quite similar unless empirically proven otherwise. Unfortunately at this time, it cannot be known whether the incidence of suicide among students with gifts and talents is different from that of the general population of adolescents (Cross, Cross, & Gong, 2009). We can, however, provide a small number of studies that begin to reveal a pattern.

In a study exploring the prevalence and nature of depression and suicidal ideation in samples of academically talented students and their nongifted peers, Baker (1995) found that the incidence of depression and suicidal ideation was similar for both gifted and nongifted adolescents. Similarly, in another study examining suicidal ideation among gifted adolescents, the gifted adolescents did not exhibit heightened rates of suicidal ideation as compared to their norm group peers (Cross, Cassady, & Miller, 2006).

Some characteristics of gifted adolescents are associated with an increased risk of suicide. Dixon and his colleagues (Dixon, Cross, Cook, & Scheckel, 1995) summarized the following characteristics that may put gifted adolescents at risk of suicide: unusual sensitivity and perfectionism (Delisle, 1986), isolationism related to extreme introversion (Kaiser & Berndt, 1985), and overexcitabilities, as identified by Dabrowski (1964, 1972). According to Delisle (1986), there are four issues making gifted adolescents susceptible to suicide attempts: perfectionism, societal expectations to achieve, differential development of intellectual and social skills, and impotence to effect real-world change. Keep in mind that there is not direct evidence to support his claim.

In most cases, gifted students have been identified for their advanced cognitive abilities. If suicide attempts begin with suicide ideation, and gifted persons have the ability or inclination to think about suicide in a different way from their nongifted peers, it is important to explore their ideation. Typical intervention methods used for nongifted adolescents may be ineffective or inappropriate for suicidal students who are gifted (Cross, 2008). Stillion, McDowell, and May (1984) found that adolescent females who scored higher on IQ tests were less likely to agree with the reasons for suicide than those with lower IQ scores. This suggests a connection between cognitive abilities and the belief that suicide is a viable solution.

Baker's (1995) efforts at understanding the unique constellation of factors that may accompany gifted and talented students' suicidal ideation have been expanded on by Cross, Cassady, and Miller (2006) and Cassady and Cross (2006). Despite the fact that both studies found rates of suicidal ideation in the gifted sample to be similar to the norm group on Reynolds' (1987) Adult Suicide Ideation Questionnaire, Cassady and Cross found that the factor structure of suicidal ideation was different in the gifted sample from the norm. Whereas Reynolds found three factors in his norm sample of adolescents—(a) wishes and plans; (b) focus on responses and aspects of others; and (c) morbid ideation— Cassady and Cross found four factors. The gifted student sample factors were (a) wishes and plans; (b) morbid fixation; (c) social isolation; and (d) social impact. Cassady and Cross acknowledged that this unique ideation pattern can provide tailored interventions for adolescents with specific risk orientations. Although how gifted individuals think about suicide requires further exploration, at this time we need to realize that students with gifts and talents engage in suicidal ideation differently than their nongifted peers.

This may have important ramifications for counseling approaches and foci.

PERSONALITY, GIFTED STUDENTS, AND SUICIDAL IDEATION

The connections between personality types and suicidal behavior are of interest to the gifted community for several reasons. Although there are no studies that clearly link giftedness to increased rates of suicide (Cross et al., 2002), it is important that concerned adults remain vigilant, nonetheless. For example, in a literature review, it was reported that half of gifted students express introverted tendencies (Sak, 2004). In another study, two of the most common at-risk types for suicide ideation included introversion (Introversion-Intuitive-Feeling-Perceiving [INFP] and Introversion-Intuitive-Thinking-Perceiving [INTP]). Moreover, given that these are common Myers-Briggs Type Indicator (MBTI) types for students who are gifted (Cross et al., 2002), there may be a high likelihood these students could experience more psychological distress and should therefore be screened for depression and/or suicidal ideation. Other common MBTI-type combinations found in gifted students include Introversion-Perceiving [IP], Introversion-Sensing-Feeling [ISF], Introversion-Intuitive-Perceiving [INP], and Extroversion-Intuitive-Judging [ENJ]. In another study, Street and Kromney (1994) have also implicated individuals with these personality characteristics who were involved in suicidal ideation or behavior. Combined, these studies suggest vigilance on our parts when we see these constellations of personality types among students with gifts and talents.

PSYCHOLOGICAL AUTOPSIES FOR FOUR STUDENTS WHO COMPLETED SUICIDE

Subsequent to the suicides at the academy (see Chapter 1), three psychological autopsies were conducted. Psychological autopsy is a case study approach to research that was begun originally to determine equivocal deaths for insurance/legal purposes. Psychological autopsy draws its data from family, friends, and significant others; family doctors; school; and the home in terms of books, music, and so forth. Interviews, records, and observations are used to gather data. The approach attempts to paint as complete a picture of the life of the student as possible. It is slow and time consuming to conduct.

After the results of the three autopsies were published, I was requested to conduct a fourth study of a gifted student who completed suicide in Vancouver. The results below represent the findings of the three in-depth studies. Following this section is a comparison of the four psychological autopsies.

COMMONALITIES WITH ADOLESCENT SUICIDE IN THE GENERAL POPULATION

I found the following commonalities between the subjects studied and adolescent suicide in the general population (Cross et al., 1996):

1. All subjects were adolescent Caucasian males.
2. All subjects manifested four emotional states:
    a. depression,
    b. anger,
    c. mood swings, and
    d. confusion about the future.

3. All manifested similar behaviors:
    a. poor impulse control, and
    b. substance use and abuse.

4. All manifested four relational difficulties:
   a. romantic relationship difficulties,
   b. self-esteem difficulties (either by exaggeration or self-condemnation),
   c. conflict-filled family relationships, and
   d. isolation from persons capable of disconfirming irrational logic.

5. The subjects shared warning signs in six categories:
   a. behavior problems,
   b. period of escalation of problems,
   c. constriction (including withdrawal from friends, dichotomous thinking),
   d. talking about suicide,
   e. changes in school performance, and
   f. family histories of psychological problems (p. 405).

COMMONALITIES AMONG THE THREE CASES RELATED TO THEIR GIFTEDNESS

I found the following commonalities related to giftedness between the subjects studied (Cross et al., 1996):

1. The subjects exhibited overexcitabilities:
   a. expressed in ways or levels beyond the norm even among their gifted peers;
   b. had minimal prosocial outlets;
   c. experienced difficulty separating fact from fiction, especially overidentification with negative asocial or aggressive characters or themes in books and movies;
   d. experienced intense emotions;
   e. felt conflicted, pained, and confused; and
   f. had difficulty with the role of emotions (e.g., one case devalued emotional experience, while two cases wanted to experience pain).

2. The subjects expressed polarized, hierarchical, egocentric value systems.
3. The subjects engaged in group theoretical discussions of suicide as a viable and honorable solution.
4. The subjects expressed behaviors consistent with Dabrowski's Level II or Level III of Positive Disintegration.
5. The subjects attended residential school as a means of escape from their family or hometown (p. 406).

When we compared the psychological autopsy of the three original intellectual gifted students who completed suicide with the fourth (Reed Ball), we found many similarities (Cross et al., 2002). Note that Reed's mother has requested that we always use his name during our research writing in lieu of traditional terms such as subject, client, deceased, and so forth. This is in an effort to enhance the cause of diminishing the stigma family members often feel after their loved one has completed suicide. The similarities we found included (Cross et al., 2002):

1. All four subjects exhibited overexcitabilities. Their overexcitabilities were expressed in ways or levels beyond the norm even among their gifted peers. The four subjects had minimal prosocial outlets. All four subjects experienced difficulty separating facts from fiction, especially overidentification with negative asocial or aggressive characters or themes in books and movies. They experienced intense emotion, felt conflicted, and wanted to rid themselves of emotions.
2. Each of the young men expressed polarized, hierarchial, egocentric value systems.
3. They each engaged in group discussions of suicide as a viable and honorable solution.
4. Additionally, all four subjects expressed behaviors consistent with Dabrowski's Level II and Level III of Positive Disintegration. (p. 252).

There were also other similarities between the fourth student and the original three (Cross et al., 2002):

> Reed was a Caucasian male who manifested four emotional characteristics: depressions, anger (represented more in suppressed rage and frustration than physical actions), mood swings and confusion about the future, while demonstrating poor impulse control (manifested more often in patterns of thought more than behavior). He experienced three relational commonalities with those in the general population who complete suicide: romantic relationship difficulties, self-esteem difficulties (either by exaggeration or self condemnation), and isolation from persons capable of disconfirming irrational logic. Reed shared warning signs in several categories: behavior problems, period of escalation of problems, constriction, withdrawal from friends, dichotomous thinking, talking about suicide, and erratic school performance. (p. 252)

Although drawing conclusions from only four case studies is risky, especially when dealing with suicide, a few important lessons can be noted. One important item is the comparison of data drawn from the students with gifts and talents with that of data from the general population. This gives us a practical tie to tried-and-true suicidal factors. In other words, predicting suicidal behavior among gifted students can be aided by research on the general population. The second lesson represents areas that seemingly are specific to students who are gifted. For example, the descriptions of overexcitabilities are believed by many to be unique among students with gifts and talents. Using Dabrowski's theory may afford suicidologists hints as to the more vulnerable among gifted students.

KEY POINTS FOR CHAPTER 5

❖ As a demographic group, students with gifts and talents are difficult to follow due to the differences in defining a gifted population.

❖ The rates of suicidal behavior of gifted and nongifted same-aged students are assumed to be quite similar unless empirically proven otherwise.

❖ Baker (1995) found that the incidence of depression and suicidal ideation was similar for both gifted and nongifted adolescents.

❖ When examining suicidal ideation among gifted adolescents, Cross et al. (2006) found that they did not exhibit heightened rates of suicidal ideation as compared to their nongifted peers.

❖ Certain characteristics, such as unusual sensitivity and perfectionism, isolationism related to extreme introversion, and overexcitabilities, may put gifted adolescents at risk of suicide.

❖ Delisle (1986) defined four issues that make gifted adolescents susceptible to suicide attempts: perfectionism, societal expectations to achieve, differential development of intellectual and social skills, and impotence to effect real-world change.

❖ Due to the ability or inclination of gifted adolescents to think about suicide in a different way from their nongifted peers, typical intervention methods may be ineffective or inappropriate for suicidal gifted students (Cross, 2008).

❖ Cassady and Cross (2006) found that the factor structure of suicidal ideation in the gifted sample was different from the three-factor structure defined by Reynolds (1987) and included (a) wishes and plans, (b) morbid fixation, (c) social isolation, and (d) social impact. This should be taken into consideration when developing counseling approaches for students with gifts and talents.

❖ Gifted students with certain introvert personality types could experience more psychological distress, are more at-risk for suicidal ideation, and, therefore, require close attention.

❖ Psychological autopsy is a case study approach to research that attempts to paint as complete a picture of the life of the student who completed suicide as possible. It draws its data from the environment and people connected to the student, and it is time consuming to conduct.

❖ Predicting suicidal behavior among students with gifts and talents can be aided by research on the general population.

CHAPTER 6

THE PERSONAL EXPERIENCE OF STUDENTS WITH GIFTS AND TALENTS

The research on the personal experience of students with gifts and talents is rich, but uneven. Coleman (2011) divided the most salient research in this area into three categories: lived experience, mixed messages, and stigma. He claimed that the three in concert make up the personal experience of gifted students (Coleman, 2011; Coleman & Cross, 2000). Personal experience becomes a very important factor when trying to understand the very complicated lives of students with gifts and talents. This also plays an important role in reconstructing the suicidal mind of this population.

Another reason this chapter exists in this book on suicide is because we can better understand the suicidal mind if we can get at personal experience. To study personal experience, phenomenology is required. Phenomenology is based on important assumptions, including the assumption that lived experience (lifeworld or lebenswelt) exists prereflectively (Husserl, 1970). This means that our experiences as people exist before we attempt to recreate them by adding labels (selecting words) to describe them. The labeling step reflects a second-order recreation of the experience, not the actual experience, and is subject to other aspects of our being. Phenomenology attempts to gain access to the lived experience of people before they start trying to recreate it with language. From this type of research, phenomenologists claim to co-create with the participants the essential elements of lived experience. In the case of suicidal behavior, studying suicide phenomenologically allows us to more fully understand the experiences and meaning that preceded the thinking about suicide (ideation) and attempts from their perspectives, not merely that of the researcher. This is consistent with Durkheim's (1951) claim that one type of extrasocial cause that influences the suicide rate is the "organic-psychic dispositions." This is also consistent with Schneidman's (1993) thinking, who, late in his career, began using increasingly phenomenologically oriented research techniques to understand suicidal behavior and specifically what preceded it. This ultimately led to his pursuit of the essential components of psychache—the central component to his theory of suicidal behavior. Other more traditional forms of research are believed by phenomenologists to be more reflective of the researcher and his or her assumptions about what is being studied rather than the actual phenomenon. Therefore, given the inherently primal nature of suicidal behavior, some suicidologists believe research into important aspects of the lives of suicidal people must be studied using phenomenology (Cross et al., 2002; Schneidman, 1993).

This chapter ties together the three aspects of the personal experience of students with gifts and talents: lived experience, mixed messages, and stigma, enabling the reader to more fully understand the complex nature of the suicidal behavior of students who are gifted. From that understanding, preventing suicide becomes more feasible.

LIVED EXPERIENCE

Much of the lived experiences of adolescents, including those who are gifted, are of a social nature and culturally situated. One's own experiences, thoughts, and feelings tend to take place in varying contexts. From being alone, to interacting with family, to attending church or school, these differing contexts tend to elicit differing experiences. Other variables such as time in history, geographic differences, gender, ethnicity, and so forth also influence experiences. Moreover, *when* students with gifts and talents have specific experiences relative to their ages (e.g., at 6 years old vs. 12 years old) is important to the phenomenology of the experiences. To make this section germane given the nature of book, I will limit the discussion to the research base of gifted students over the past 25 years in the U.S., as related to school.

As a young gifted child grows, being identified as gifted or not being identified as gifted matters in his or her experiences. Being known as gifted tends to have roles and expectations ascribed to it. Many of these roles and expectations would not be true for non-identified or nongifted students. For example, Cross, Stewart, and Coleman (2003) described students who are gifted speaking out about their lives in school:

> They spoke of being embarrassed when held up as examples for other students; confused when students taunted them; and upset when told by the teacher that he or she was disappointed in them due to a test score, incorrectly answering a question in class, or any number of other "failures." (p. 4)

The expectations placed on our students with gifts and talents are perceived early and become a screen through which growing up is filtered. Many will become successful students while developing a passion for learning (Coleman, 2011). Some will underachieve and experience considerable disappointment from others. Some will internalize their value as directly reflective of their accomplishments in school. Still others will minimize the expectations of themselves relative to school and hold higher expectations for their work in their local communities. This type of commitment can be seen in myriad examples ranging from students who are active in church, gangs, or anything in between. In essence, the lived experience of gifted students establishes the foundations of the person's identity.

MIXED MESSAGES

I'm different you know; you show intelligence and your outspoken, and people tend to isolate you and put a label on you. (Cross et al., 2003, p. 203)

Students who are gifted in Western societies grow up experiencing unique expressions of mixed messages. In many countries, giftedness itself is widely argued about with little agreement as to its definition. Within professional organizations, participants often maintain tacit definitions of giftedness based upon their involvement with their students. Within families there are quite often wide variations of the definition and meaning of giftedness. Constant topics such as elitism, or whether giftedness is merely an asset, engender considerable and often strongly held beliefs about giftedness. Longstanding models of schooling have historically been based on keeping children of similar ages together, and thereby keeping children of similar intellectual capacity apart. This fact has contributed to concerns about the potential harm to children when certain gifted education recommendations are put into place such as grade skipping, early admission, or any other recommendations for acceleration (Southern & Jones, 1991). Educational legislation such as the No Child Left Behind Act (NCLB) of 2001 has forced school districts to focus their attention on students just within reach of a performance band, while paying increasingly less attention to those who had already surpassed that relatively low band of expectations. NCLB created conditions for an entire generation of students with gifts and talents, that their actual performance in school was not valued, especially if they demonstrated mastery of the minimum competency test. Ironically, in their classic book that provides a critical view of our schools, Howley, Howley, and Pendarvis (1995), years before NCLB was implemented, concluded that many of the schools in the U.S. are actually anti-intellectual environments.

As every culture creates expectations for its people based on gender, race, ethnicity, socioeconomic groupings, religion, and so forth, students who are gifted also must figure out what being a gifted student means. They learn of society members' prejudices, general expectations, and academic expectations. The must live within their family and community rules, while feeling pressure to live up to their potential. Each teacher has tacit assumptions about gifted students that will play out in the student's life in real time. At the same time, students with gifts and talents, like all students, are developing as people and are dealing with psychosocial developmental issues such as making friends, dating, and so forth. The myriad mixed messages add considerable conflict to these issues.

A recent conflicting trend, the emphasis on increasing the number of students moving into science, technology, engineering, and math (STEM), adds further fuel to the mixed messages that these students receive. Over the past quarter century, the professional organizations in gifted education (National Association for Gifted Children, The Association for the Gifted) have emphasized a multitude of talent domains in which students can and should develop talent. The effects of the recent federal emphasis and considerable funding for students to pursue careers in STEM has narrowed considerably the options for gifted students and sent the clear message that other talent domains are not valued. These examples reflect the wide-ranging and deeply held philosophical differences of people in society that end up being internalized by gifted students. Because of this fact, and the need to exist socially in school, students with gifts and talents create coping strategies for navigating the social waters of family, school, community, and so forth (Coleman & Cross, 1988).

Stigma of Giftedness

In 1985, Coleman developed a Stigma of Giftedness Paradigm (SGP) based on the classic book by Erving Goffman (1963) entitled *Stigma: Notes on the Management of Spoiled Identity*. Falk (2001) claimed that there are two categories of stigma, existential and achieved. Existential stigma was defined as stigma deriving from a condition which the target of the stigma either did not cause or over which he has little control. Achieved stigma is earned because of conduct and/or because they contributed heavily to attaining the stigma in question. (p. 11)

Existential stigma is the type of stigma that the SGP attempts to illustrate. To that end, the SGP has three tenets:

1. Students who are gifted want to have normal social interactions. Note that "normal" is idiosyncratic. (Each person determines his or her goal for normal.)
2. Gifted students learn that when others learn of their giftedness, they will treat the gifted students differently. (Not necessarily worse, merely differently than they would have been treated had this fact remained unknown.)
3. They realize they can manage information about themselves that others are allowed to have. (Families often teach their children to behave differently across settings, including sharing information about oneself judiciously.)

Several studies based on the SGP (e.g., Coleman & Cross, 1988; Cross, Coleman, & Stewart, 1993; Cross, Coleman, & Terhaar-Yonkers, 1991) have been conducted. Each study has demonstrated that students who are gifted and talented attend schools that are complicated social environments, so complicated that Tannenbaum (1983) opined:

There is evidence to show that the gifted are influenced by their peers', parents' and teachers' feelings about their abilities. If they are seen as mental freaks, unhealthy personalities, or eccentric simply because they are brainy or creative, many of them will avoid the stigma through conformity. Some would rather underachieve and be popular than achieve honor status and receive ostracism. (p. 466).

Research has documented that gifted students engage in myriad social coping strategies (Coleman & Cross, 1988; Cross et al., 1991; Cross et al., 1993; Cross & Swiatek, 2009) to exist comfortably in their school. The strategies reveal the concerns of the student relative to gaining the social interactions they desire. For example, students who are gifted tend to have one of three goals for their social lives while in school. Coleman and Cross (1988) created a Continuum of Visibility that illustrates the three goals: standing out, invisibility, and disidentifying. When students who are gifted desire to stand out, to be known as being gifted, they engage in social coping behaviors that bring attention to themselves for their giftedness. To that end, they answer numerous questions during a single class period, talk about their accomplishments or test scores or any of a large number of attention-getting behaviors, or dress the part of a scientist. Students with gifts and talents who desire to become invisible or blend in do so by wearing clothes that are common to their schoolmates, answer few questions during class, sit quietly, protect their successful test scores from other students, and so forth. These behaviors keep them from standing out. The third group (disidentifiers) is not satisfied with standing out or blending in, they want to be disassociated with other gifted and talented students. To do so, they hang around with other groups of students stereotyped to be made up of nongifted students. Common groups mentioned when students who are gifted describe this behavior include druggies, emos, skateboarders, and goths. These groups will vary across schools. The strategy is based on the student identifying, within the social milieu of the school, the groups that are stereotyped to be comprised of nongifted students. This is despite that fact that gifted students tend to exist in virtually all groups of any school. Some girls claimed that, as a strategy for disidentifying, they would go on a date with a boy thought to be "dumb." Other students go out for activities for which they have no talent. Students with gifts and talents have many social coping strategies, no matter to which of the three goals they aspire (standing out, blending in, or disidentifying).

Given the complicated social environments of our schools (that in many cases are anti-intellectual in nature), plus the pervasive mixed messages received, what does the mind of students with gifts and talents include? For example, how do these complicating factors affect the psychological well-being of gifted students? How do they affect the behaviors of this population? How might they contribute to the suicidal ideation of gifted students? Combined with characteristics of individual students who are gifted, how does the confluence of these variables affect these students as it pertains to suicidal behavior?

KEY POINTS FOR CHAPTER 6

* ❖ The personal experience of SWGT is divided into three categories: lived experience, mixed messages, and stigma (Coleman, 2011). Studying these three aspects together will allow us to better understand the complex nature of gifted students' suicidal behavior and may help prevent suicide.

* ❖ When researching suicidal behavior of students, the phenomenological approach allows us to more fully understand the experiences and meaning that preceded the ideation and attempts from the students' perspectives.

* ❖ Much of the lived experiences of all adolescents, including those who are gifted, are of a social nature and culturally situated.

* ❖ The lived experience of students with gifts and talents establishes the foundations of the person's identity.

* ❖ NCLB created conditions for an entire generation of gifted students such that their actual performance in school was not valued, especially if they have demonstrated mastery of the minimum competency test.

* ❖ Students who are gifted must figure out what being a gifted student means in their society and culture: They must live by their family and societal rules, while at the same time living up to their potential.

❖ Gifted students create coping strategies in order to fit in and deal with a multitude of mixed messages.

❖ In 1985, Coleman developed a Stigma of Giftedness Paradigm and attempted to illustrate existential stigma (i.e., stigma derived from a condition that the target of the stigma either did not cause or over which he has little control).

❖ Coleman and Cross (1988) created a Continuum of Visibility that illustrates the three goals students who are gifted set themselves as a way of coping with complex social lives while in school: standing out, blending in, and disidentifying.

CHAPTER 7

TOWARD A MODEL OF SUICIDAL BEHAVIOR FOR STUDENTS WITH GIFTS AND TALENTS

Over the years that I have pondered the suicidal mind and behavior of students with gifts and talents, I have considered the traditional research about suicide of the general population. I have considered contextual and historical influences and, finally, the actual research on the suicide of students with gifts and talents. My research conducting psychological autopsies caused me to see developmental aspects of suicidal behavior and the need to investigate the essence of lived experience of the suicidal mind. As I learned that Schneidman had come to a similar conclusion fairly late in his career, I gained the confidence to make these aspects foundational to my model. Moreover, I have found Schneidman's (1993) work most compelling in its rich description of the primal experience of psychache.

This synthesis of information has led to the development of the spiral model of the suicidal mind of gifted children and adolescents. The model attempts to build on both Schneidman's (1993) work and the STM by Stillion and McDowell (1996). Conceptually, combined with gifted-specific research and observations, these two theories provide a comprehensive foundation that has the benefits of both the empirically validated research reflecting the general population and the fine distinctions needed to anticipate and understand the suicidal mind of students with gifts and talents.

The spiral model of the suicidal mind of gifted children and adolescents will be described conceptually below and illustrated to assist with the explanations. It builds from the model categories and risk factors of the STM along with the more phenomenological aspects of Schneidman's (1993) theory, to the more nuanced, empirically based ideas from the research on suicidal behavior of gifted students. For context, however, before I present the spiral model, I will provide a two-dimensional illustration of a triangle (see Figure 3) based on the Stillion and McDowell (1996) and Schneidman (1993) theories, plus the research about gifted students and suicide. Subsequently, I present the spiral model, which attempts to provide a three-dimensional image of the interactions of all of the factors provided to date, including those specific to students who are gifted.

The bottom fourth of the triangle includes the four categories of the suicide trajectory model (see Table 12 for a reminder of what those categories entail). The correlates and risk factors of suicidal behavior establish the foundation of the suicidal mind. However, many people function well even with many of the suicidal correlates.

The STM establishes an excellent foundation of risk factors from which to look for and predict suicidal behavior. The four categories are comprehensive, including biological traits/characteristics (e.g., being male), psychological characteristics (e.g., mood states), negative cognitive patterns (e.g., self-talk), and environmental factors (e.g., social isolation and exposure to lethal weapons). These factors are at a level that educators could be trained to identify as a means to reduce the likelihood of suicidal behavior.

The next level of the triangle includes factors identified from research on the suicidal behavior of students with gifts and talents. Isolation, feeling different, lived experience, mixed messages, and others are layered on top of the factors of the STM.

The third tier of the triangle includes the elements within Schneidman's (1993) theory. He described suicide as having four

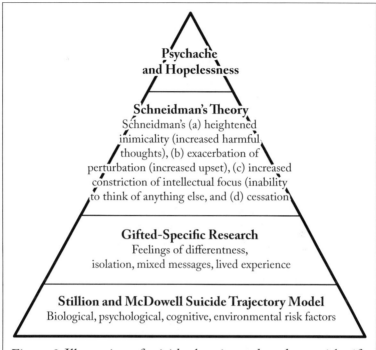

Figure 3. Illustration of suicide theories and students with gifts and talents leading to spiral model.

elements: (a) heightened inimicality, (b) exacerbation of perturbation, (c) increased constriction of intellectual focus, and (d) cessation. From the STM, we can now see how the process of the suicidal mind is becoming actively involved. As suicidal ideators increase their harmful thoughts and become more and more upset, they become less able to think about anything else. The only discernable solution is cessation: death. Factors associated with suicide can be considered kinetic, and Schneidman's theory (1993) illustrates how the factors become activated or engaged.

As the person becomes increasingly involved in suicidal ideation, the factors noted in the STM such as rigidity of thought exacerbate the perturbation (increases the upset) that Schneidman (1993) described. This is where the two most important states can have the effect of preparing the person to die: psychache and hope-

Table 12
Suicide Trajectory Model Categories and Associated Risk Factors

Category	Risk Factors
Biological	Gender (male) Race (Native American, White) Genetic bases (parental psychopathy) Sexual orientation (homosexual, bisexual) Serotonin dysfunction
Psychological	Low self-esteem Depressed mood Feelings of hopelessness/helplessness Aggressive-impulsive tendencies Poor coping strategies Existential questions
Cognitive	Poor social problem solving Inflexible thinking Negative self-talk Rigidity of thought
Environmental	Familial dysfunction (Impaired parent-child relationships) Social isolation Stressful life circumstances (interpersonal loss) Presence of lethal methods Exposure to suicide completers (friends/family)

lessness. As a person experiences increasing amounts of psychological and emotional pain, the variable of hopelessness becomes more and more important.

Risk factors can be considered distally related to suicide, while warning signs such as psychache and hopelessness are thought to be proximally associated with a suicidal behavior and related to imminent risk. Distal causes are believed to be the initial causative factors in the original environment, while proximal causes are current causative factors.

These proximal causes can be seen at the top of the triangle, in Schneidman's (1993) psychache and the construct of hopelessness. The two states of mind are much closer to potential suicidal behavior than any of the correlates. However, the correlates provide fuel for the psychache that leads to hopelessness, which in turn leads to suicidal behavior.

SPIRAL MODEL OF THE SUICIDAL MIND OF GIFTED CHILDREN AND ADOLESCENTS

Building on the theories and research represented in the triangle in Figure 3, I have developed the spiral model of the suicidal mind of gifted children and adolescents, shown in Figure 4. The image of the spiral was chosen as a good metaphor for the life of people and how differing events, circumstances, and protective factors battle to keep each person spiraling high above the destruction on the ground before one crashes through and dies. The image allows for important details to be shown as weights or protective factors.

The swirling around at the top of the spiral illustrates the movement in one's life in a relatively flat plane of positive mental health. An individual's path dips with events and circumstances in life that cause high levels of upset, anxiety, or distress, but remains in a generally positive trajectory along the top. Negative effects on the mental health plane of the top spiral tend to be episodic for most people. Those people with bipolar disorder, for example, experience extreme emotional swings, and would reflect that in their image of the spiral, with many dips along the top plane. Others' patterns, while idiosyncratic, would tend to reflect a relatively consistent plane, indicating the ability to deal effectively with life's struggles.

Just as a tornado moves, a person is moving, developing over time. The height of the spiral is meant to reflect the distance one is from suicide, or, stated differently, a person's level of mental health. The width of the body of the spiral reveals the speed of life as one experiences it.

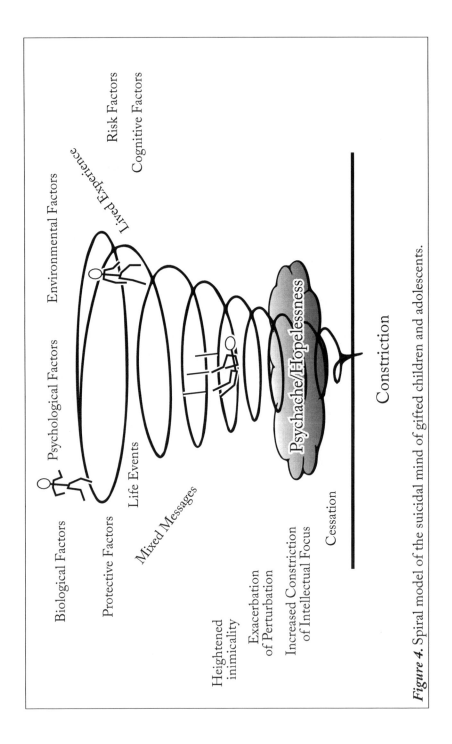

Figure 4. Spiral model of the suicidal mind of gifted children and adolescents.

A way to imagine this is to assume that this model of mental health represents the life of a person across her or his lifespan. For some, the spiral lasts 85 years or more, while others die at birth. For those who survive birth, many of the protective factors are present, such as biological controls of breathing, hunger, and so forth. The image of a newborn actually illustrates the early indicators of the importance of relationships with others to the mental health of a person as he or she grows into adulthood. More specifically, if the child is not fed, then he or she dies. If he or she is not changed regularly or is neglected, then he or she fails to resolve a psychosocial crisis (i.e., trust vs. mistrust) and develops an important psychosocial doubt that is carried through life (Erikson, 1963). As the young person develops, increasing numbers and types of protective factors are also developing. For example, love for family and friends, identity formation, development of agency, sense of industry, and many more are added to the biological predispositions that help keep a person safe. Belief systems that make suicide taboo can also be helpful in keeping people alive.

In sum, the spiral serves as a reasonable vehicle on which to place the numerous biological, psychological, cognitive, and environmental risk factors of Stillion and McDowell's (1996) theory. The same is true for Schneidman's (1993) psychological constructs of heightened inimicality, exacerbation of perturbation, increased constriction of intellectual focus, and cessation. Combined, these two theories establish a solid foundation to which we can add the gifted-specific issues, concerns, and phenomenological factors. In addition, Table 10 (see p. 24–25) provided a representation of both the factors associated with suicidal behavior and protections against it. If you consider it the backdrop for the spiral, it is easy to imagine how the person can be influenced over time.

The problem emerges when a person gets knocked out of his or her spiral that is parallel to the ground. Myriad life events such as divorce, moving, illness, death of family members, and relationship problems are noted by Stillion and McDowell (1996) to cause this. In most cases, the protective factors such as those in Table 10 illustrate why we tend to bounce back, regaining our symmetrical orbit, parallel to and above the ground. Drugs and alcohol, depression, or other comorbid psychological issues are examples of factors associated with suicidal behavior. These can be seen in Stillion and McDowell's (1996) and Gould et al.'s (2003) work. As illustrative as these correlates and risk factors are, I believe that it takes hopelessness and Schneidman's (1993) psychache to break through the protective factors that keep us safe from suicide. The intense psychological pain and hopelessness makes a person quite susceptible to efforts at eliminating the overwhelming, inescapable pain—suicide attempts.

The spiral, with the issues and factors from research on students with gifts and talents, provides a visual aid in understanding the suicidal mind of the child or adolescent. For example, we have learned that the factor structure of suicidal ideation among gifted adolescents is different from that of their nongifted peers (Cassady & Cross, 2006) and that gifted adolescents reveal some personality types (introversion and perceptive) that are more closely associated with suicidal ideation than the general population (Cross et al., 2006). Although these two examples are important, the research needs to be replicated with expanded samples of students with gifts and talents.

Research on the personal experience of giftedness suggests that gifted and talented students receive mixed messages abut their giftedness (Coleman & Cross, 1988), often grow up in anti-intellectual environments (Howley et al., 1995), believe that they are different from others (Cross et al., 1993), perceive a stigma of giftedness (Coleman, 1985), and create social coping behaviors (Coleman & Cross, 1988; Cross & Swiatek, 2009) to create a level of comfort within their schools. The internalization of these influences on the identity of gifted students adds to their negative self-images, creating a lack of confidence and self-doubt. Moreover, the simple fact is that extraordinary minds have few peers. Combined, these factors can lead to anxiety, isolation, alienation, and depression—correlates of suicidal behavior.

KEY POINTS FOR CHAPTER 7

❖ The spiral model of the suicidal mind of gifted students builds from the model categories and risk factors of the Suicide Trajectory Model (STM) to the more phenomenological aspects of Schneidman's (1993) theory, to the more nuanced, empirically based ideas from the research on suicidal behavior of students with gifts and talents.

❖ The factors of the STM are generally at a conceptual level that professional educators could be trained to identify, and in many cases work with, to reduce the likelihood of suicidal behavior.

❖ The next level of the spiral model is Schneidman's (1993) theory, illustrating how the factors associated with suicide become activated or engaged.

❖ Risk factors can be thought to be distally related to suicide, while warning signs such as psychache and hopelessness are thought to be proximally associated with suicidal behavior and related to potential imminent risk.

CHAPTER 8

PREVENTING SUICIDE AMONG STUDENTS WITH GIFTS AND TALENTS

A SCHOOL-BASED APPROACH

To help prevent the suicides of students with gifts and talents by their own hand, I will focus on the contribution that schools can make. The primary reason to focus on schools is because virtually all of these students attend schools and therefore can be reached within this institution. A second reason for the school-based emphasis is the fact that schools have considerable resources to bring to bear. There is also the invaluable potential of peers and faculty and staff to provide important services on behalf of the potentially suicidal student. The final reason is that schools are replete with friendship groups. I have found that other students often have information about a potentially suicidal student before the adults do. For a comprehensive system to be created, all of these groups must participate.

To be most effective, schools need to create an overt plan that includes a steering committee representing all of the stakeholders. The plan should delineate specific goals and objectives that can be measured from year to year to prevent slippage with the influx of new students and the change in school personnel. The goals and objectives should be established for each stakeholder group. Ideally, the suicide prevention plan would be a significant part of an overarching plan to create a caring community.

Caring communities attempt to help all students thrive in all aspects of their school lives. To begin, thriving must be defined. From its definition, indicators can be developed. For example, thriving might be defined as "students will demonstrate psychological well-being, appropriate levels of academic achievement, and reasonable levels of physical fitness." The metrics used to consider these areas would be both normative and idiosyncratic. This guarantees that both a sociological and individual perspective can be had. Because suicidal behavior is both predicted by environmental and phenomenological factors, both perspectives are needed to prevent it.

To reach the goals and objectives established, information will have to be understood and internalized, and behaviors will have to be changed. To that end, significant ongoing training will have to be conducted. The training would be tailored for the various stakeholder groups and at varying degrees of sophistication. For example, because everything planned would be under the goal of thriving, some specific knowledge about the suicide of gifted students would necessarily be included strategically for the greatest impact.

In addition to the three basic goals established to create a caring community in which everyone thrives, officials would also need to identify characteristics and expectations. Some characteristics might include open communication, personal responsibility, community responsibility, candor, and no bullying. Other aspects of a caring community wherein everyone thrives is the inclusion of stakeholders across decision-making groups in an effort to share power. Moreover, the most important outcome of these factors should be the creation of trust. Trust provides a guarantee that a caring community can exist and be maintained. An important underpinning of a caring community is that the adults will be appropriately trained to gain enough knowledge and expertise to provide the awareness, guidance, and decision making needed to create a safe, caring community. Good will, absent of significant training, can actually contribute to a less safe environment. For

Table 13
Common Myths Associated With Suicide and Gifted Students

Myth #1	Suicide occurs without warning.
Myth #2	Gifted and talented youths who talk about suicide are not serious about committing suicide.
Myth #3	Educating gifted students about suicide can lead to an increase in suicide ideation among this population coupled with more knowledge about ways of being successful in their suicide attempts.
Myth #4	If a gifted young person wants to commit suicide, very little can stop her or him.
Myth #5	Only trained counselors or mental health professionals are capable of intervening with suicidal gifted youths.

example, adults are prone to believe some of myths associated with suicide and gifted students (King, 1997), like those in Table 13.

Many of these myths are widely held and counter to helping create a caring community wherein all students, including those who are gifted, thrive. Education of the realities about suicide must be taught and school employees will need to be held accountable to know them. In this chapter, I refute these myths while offering a plan for schools to prevent the suicidal behavior of students with gifts and talents.

I have found that an effective way to create comfort among educators relative to suicide is to reduce their self-imposed expectations that they need to be able to evaluate the potential for imminent harm. This expectation hurts on two fronts: some educators tend to believe that no student is that serious about suicide, while other educators avoid any contact with the issue. By reducing the educator's expectation that they cannot become expert enough to discern the potential for imminent harm, as that is the domain of a clinical psychologist or psychiatrist (for the most part), to the goal of merely noticing students in distress, they tend to become willing to become part of a team trying to reduce suicidal behavior. Most educators develop quite an eye for noticing students in distress and the additional training helps them know how to expand their knowledge while at the same time learning about additional steps that they can take to be helpful. Many educators fear suicide to such an extent that they avoid getting involved. Others do not know what to do. And a small group worries about being made a fool by students trying to manipulate them. By emphasizing the goal of discerning distress in students, educators feel more comfortable and become more active in the process.

Therefore, educators and students would receive training in the basics about suicide, including its definition, prevalence rates, correlates, factors, and so forth among the general population. Ideally, this would include parents as well. School administrators and counselors would be trained in the most current knowledge about suicide and students with gifts and talents. Teachers would receive important information about suicide, gifted students, and distress and what to do next. This information might emphasize identifying distress and making referrals.

Other schoolwide information would include the importance of helping and the fact that suicide can be prevented, even among those who are already suicidal. In some cases, mantras can be helpful. For example, the group most knowledgeable in schools about students in distress is the students. Adults often overlook many of these students. Consequently, including students in organizing and steering committees will help in the creation of effective communication processes that lead to trust. Without this element, the school environment will not be as safe. A cross current that sometimes exists in schools is that students will come to think that telling adults that someone they know is struggling would be "ratting them out." And in some environments, ratting someone out is to be avoided at all costs. These environments could benefit from the mantra that it is better to have a live enemy than a dead friend (Cross et al., 1996). I have used this technique with great success.

Part of the training for all groups is the concept that, to be a caring community, a school must be made up of people who see the value of helping the school reach the goals set for it. Of course, this can take many forms and cut across a large number of areas.

For example, in addition to the mental health aspect of the school, academics, sports, and other extracurricular aspects of the school can be pursued. Nutrition and exercise are important to all of the aforementioned goals, but are seldom included in this process. As noted, an essential aspect to obtaining support across all groups is the inclusion of all groups in the process. Consequently, pulling everything under the diversity topic makes good sense here. Because schools tend to be microcosms of communities, they tend to reflect considerable diversity. When aspects of diversity that are salient in schools are added to the mix, then the stakeholder groups should take on the form of the diversity represented. This inclusionary practice bodes well for the creation of a caring community and one wherein trust is the defining characteristic. Expertise becomes utilized to facilitate myriad groups ranging from educational needs, to needs around ethnicity, to mental health matters. All are respected as part of the community, and none are held in disdain, contempt, or fear. Implicit in a caring community is the need to also be a learning community. To function in the increasingly complicated world, it is essential that all parties continue their educations. This aspect of the caring community guarantees the trust and high levels of expertise needed to address serious problems such as preventing suicides. When absent from the numerous aspects of the caring community described, suicide prevention is treated in such a manner that tends to further isolate people while exacerbating distrust.

Several recommendations involve modifications or additions to the school curriculum. Schools may wish to consider including a unit on suicide prevention as a part of the mental health curriculum, beginning as early as junior high school. The mental health curriculum should consider strategies that incorporate common needs of students, including their need for acceptance, companionship, and self-understanding. Students play a crucial role in recognizing other adolescents who are suicidal (Delisle, 1990), and the more educated they are about suicide, the more of an asset they become. Eckert, Miller, DuPaul, and Riley-Tillman (2003) described curriculum programs for students that attempt to (a) heighten awareness regarding suicide, (b) train them to recognize signs of suicidal behavior in order to help others, and (c) provide students with information about various school and community resources. Although research suggests proceeding cautiously when implementing suicide curriculum programs, it has been shown to be an effective approach for intervening in school settings (Eckert et al., 2003).

Reynolds's model (as discussed in Eckert et al., 2003) includes a two-stage screening and assessment process. The process identifies potentially suicidal students and could be used as schoolwide practice for suicide prevention. In the first stage, a classwide or schoolwide screening takes place, in which all students complete a brief self-report measure to identify those who may be at risk for suicide. The second stage involves doing individual interviews with all students who score above clinically significant levels. Although promising, the acceptability of this technique is questionable (Eckert et al., 2003). This is due to the fact that screening tools tend to report false positives for some young people while missing others who are at risk. Consequently, educators are encouraged to employ a screening tool more than once.

Schools involved in suicide prevention should create an environment that promotes and reinforces positive social relationships (Fleith, 1998). In this setting, students feel comfortable sharing their concerns and are encouraged to dream and use their imaginations. In essence, according to Fleith (2001), schools should encourage activities that nurture students' interests, strengths, and abilities.

Suicidologists representing the dominant paradigm claim that suicidal behavior is not evidence of youths working through difficulties in their life. Rather, it is illustrative of people struggling with some form of mental illness (Pelkonen & Marttunen, 2003). This is an important consideration when deciding what facets to include in a schoolwide suicide prevention program. He goes on to claim that that describing suicide as a reasonable response to adolescent problems could inadvertently facilitate the expression of suicidal ideas. Consequently, educators must be aware of the potential to contribute to the idea that suicide is a viable option when experiencing stress.

School-based prevention programs risk alienating those students considering suicide by sending messages that can be misconstrued as equating suicidal ideation with mental illness. Although it is important to challenge students who ideate about suicide, other students might go underground and not pursue the help they need. These issues illustrate the importance of effective communication across the various stakeholder groups when implementing this type of school-based intervention.

The importance of creating a caring community in school cannot be overstated. Myriad mental health issues are prevented, improved upon, and/or effectively monitored with the appropriate referrals made. The day-to-day activities of the stakeholders are carried out among community members who are dedicated to every person's wellness. People look after each other, feeling a personal responsibility. All stakeholder groups have considerable knowledge about distress, depression, frustration, and suicidal behavior. This type of environment creates protective factors that can help prevent suicidal behavior. All schools should create a caring community—the accumulation of benefits to the well-being of their students will be staggering when they do. To prevent suicides among students who are gifted, we must collaborate by drawing on the most up-to-date research available. This book can be used to begin the process of education about suicidal behavior in general and among our students with gifts and talents more specifically.

KEY POINTS FOR CHAPTER 8

❖ Schools can help prevent the suicide of students for a number of reasons: all students attend schools and can be reached within the institution; schools have considerable resources; schools have an invaluable potential of peers, faculty, and staff to provide important services on behalf of the potentially suicidal student; and schools are replete with friendship groups.

❖ To be most effective, schools need to create an overt plan that includes a steering committee representing all of the stakeholders.

❖ Ideally, the suicide prevention plan would be a significant part of an overarching plan to create a caring community.

❖ Good will, absent of significant training, can actually contribute to a less safe environment, which is why adults in the caring community should be appropriately trained.

❖ One of the common myths associated with suicide and gifted students is that suicide occurs without warning.

❖ The realities about suicide must be taught and school employees will need to be held accountable to know them.

❖ An effective way to create comfort among educators relative to suicide is to reduce their self-imposed expectations that they need to be able to evaluate the potential for imminent harm.

❖ Including students in organizing and steering committees will help in the creation of effective communication processes and a safe school environment.

❖ It is better to have a live enemy than a dead friend.

❖ Schools may wish to consider including a unit on suicide prevention as a part of the mental health curriculum, beginning as early as junior high school.

❖ Researchers and clinicians representing the dominant paradigm among suicidologists claim that suicidal behavior is not evidence of youths working through difficulties in their life, but of young people struggling with some form of mental illness.

❖ Myriad mental health issues are prevented, improved upon, and effectively monitored with the appropriate referrals made.

❖ To prevent suicides among students who are gifted, we must collaborate by drawing on the most up-to-date research available.

CHAPTER 9

HEALING THE SUICIDAL MIND OF STUDENTS WITH GIFTS AND TALENTS

Healing a suicidal mind is very difficult and not always successful. There are myriad factors that influence the potential for success. Some of those include access to mental health professionals and the type and degree of comorbid factors. Should a person be determined to be potentially suicidal, assessing his or her risk of imminent harm is often the first step of treatment. The goals for assisting a person believed to be at this level of distress are simple and direct: keep him or her alive. Typically this leads to in-house care at a residential facility that specializes in serious mental health care. Those admitted often stay for 48–72 hours. They must be reevaluated for the potential of imminent harm before they can be released. In a perfect world, they remain as an outpatient receiving appropriate psychological care on an outpatient basis. The treatment often includes both talk and pharmaceutical therapy. Psychologists tend to provide the talk therapy while psychiatrists arrange the medications. Other combinations can also exist, such as clinical social workers, or other professionals licensed at the master's degree level, who are supervised by licensed doctoral-level psychologists or psychiatrists. Specific techniques for therapy will vary based on the philosophical underpinnings of the training received by the psychologist providing the therapy.

Once the person is out of imminent harm, or if he or she were never in immediate harm, the most highly recommended approach includes both counseling and medication (if called for). One without the other, when both are recommended, is believed to be an inferior approach to treatment. Although describing a typical acute care notion of healing a suicidal mind is important, it is out of the hands of those who work in schools. Moreover, care after a person who is suicidal is inherently ameliorative. Much of this work is best done by professionals. Therefore, the remainder of this book will emphasize ideas for assisting in the positive development of the psychology of students with gifts and talents.

In the Presence of a Suicidal Individual

We know that a person in imminent danger of harming him- or herself should be placed in the care of professionals. Once a person is identified as suicidal and receiving appropriate psychological care, he or she should be among the professionals who can save him or her for the short term and help him or her move from suicidal to stable. But many of the situations in which those of us who work or live with gifted students find ourselves are more ambiguous. How does a teacher who spots a student whose work is laced with death-related images or who appears self-loathing respond? When is it time to seek support from a professional? How does one act in the moment when faced with a depressed child? How can we create an environment that supports positive development, so the pain of psychache never enters?

To foster an environment where psychache cannot exist, adults must be on the lookout for students in psychological pain. As my Spiral Model suggests, adults should be wary of life events that can throw their students with gifts and talents off the plane of positive mental functioning. Transition points, such as a move from elementary to middle school or middle school to high school, family moves that result in many changes, divorce, and death of a loved one (even a pet) are all precipitating events that can upset the balance on the plane of positive function. Those with predisposing or contributing factors (see Table 10) should receive special attention. Adolescents who have made previous attempts or those who have poor coping skills may not be able to hoist themselves up from the lower levels of the spiral. Adults and peers can provide the support that is required, but concern for the individual is a necessary ingredient for success. A second ingredient is knowledge about what to do. It is important not to minimize students' reaction to a situation. Their perspective must be taken seriously, or they will not feel supported. It can help to work on their perceptions of a situation, but an adult's belief in the insignificance of the problem will not be helpful in doing so.

Peers can be a primary source of support, but it is extremely important to help them recognize their limitations. It is unfair to burden a peer with the responsibility of keeping a friend from falling into hopelessness. The responsibility he or she feels for the life of a peer is likely to go far beyond that an adult would feel. In order to respond appropriately, young people and adults alike must have proper education. What should someone say to a friend who expresses suicidal thoughts? When is it necessary to bring an adult into the situation? What adult is the right one? All schools should have at least one contact person who is sympathetic and trusted by students and educated in the steps to take in the case of a suicidal child. All adults, including parents, should be trained in appropriate interventions—how to recognize a suicidal student, what to say, who to report it to, and when to report it. No one can be apathetic or the slide down the spiral will continue unimpeded.

CREATING A POSITIVE ENVIRONMENT FOR STUDENTS WITH GIFTS AND TALENTS

In this section, I will shed light on the lived experiences of gifted students with an emphasis on helping them thrive psychologically in the school environment. There are unique factors that may increase protection or risk for these students, depending on how they are experienced in context.

When growing up gifted, there are several areas of development in which the gifted person's endogenous characteristics (those within the person) encounter the exogenous characteristics of differing environments. Some early examples include being an early reader, developing an impressive vocabulary, developing early advanced computer skills, beginning school early, and so forth. As the very young gifted student encounters these challenges to norms, he or she often deviates from them and rubs up against stereotypes and tacit values of the other students and faculty. Consequently, depending upon the level of maturation of the gifted child's social cognition, he or she will begin the process of determining to what extent the school environment is supportive or hostile. In the mind of a young gifted child, he or she will not have the maturity that comes with experience and age to make informed decisions about complex social situations. This can cause young gifted children to internalize all sorts of mixed messages about giftedness and themselves.

As they progress in school, the degree to which the school environment is an anti-intellectual environment will have an effect on a gifted student's feelings of potential stigmatization. Many will develop social coping behaviors to try to create and maintain the social latitude they desire. The social coping behaviors can range from somewhat neutral behavior like sitting quietly, to underachieving. The net effect of experiencing mixed messages and anti-intellectual environments is the feeling of being different or aberrant.

When students with gifts and talents mature, being gifted is part of who they are as people. For many, it is very much a defining part of their identity. In schools that take academic matters seriously, they can thrive. Unfortunately, many of our schools are, in fact, anti-intellectual settings (Howley et al., 1995). It should be noted that the size of school matters here—larger urban and suburban schools create social environments that are not very porous. Moving between groups can get difficult, so many students with gifts and talents employ social coping strategies that can have negative impacts on their academic success. For example, underachievement or going underground can be the result of strategies for blending in or disidentifying.

Meanwhile, all of the typical developmental issues that affect school-aged children are also affecting gifted students. Giftedness becomes another way that the students appear nonmodal in the eyes of others, and in their own self-assessment. During adolescence, fitting in and standing out are often desired at the same time. Other examples of adolescent issues include wanting to be special while needing to feel the same as other students or feeling like one does not have any intellectual peers close to one's same age. Because many schools seem to value sports more than academics, the groups with the lowest social status in many secondary schools are nonathletes who are studious (Cramond & Martin, 1987). These examples make friendship formation difficult and often lead to limited prosocial outlets, a common finding in psychological autopsies of gifted students who killed themselves (Cross et al., 2002).

I have come to believe that the most pervasive threat to mental health of gifted students in school is the mismatch between the school's curriculum and the students' academic needs. Attending schools for years and constantly having this experience creates all sorts of problems for them. Although I have never actually seen a school that creates learning conditions wherein all students, including those who are gifted, operate at 100% capacity day in and day out, I estimate that many students who are gifted operate at less than 50% of their capacity for many years of their educational careers. This can be very frustrating for students with gifts and talents.

Over the years I have created a number of recommendations that I believe help raise a well-adjusted gifted child. To the extent we can do this, the less we will contribute to creating suicidal behaviors. Erik Erikson's (1963) Theory of Psychosocial Development is one of the most important theories in psychology and was the first to illustrate how people continue to develop

Table 14
Erikson's (1963) Theory of Psychosocial Development Stages of Crisis

Age	Crisis to be resolved	Virtue
Birth to 1 year	Trust vs. Mistrust	Hope
1 to 3 years	Autonomy vs. Shame and Doubt	Will
3 to 6 years (pre-K–1)	Initiative vs. Guilt	Purpose
6 to 12 years (grades 1–6)	Industry vs. Inferiority	Competence
12 to 20 years (grades 7+)	Identity vs. Role Confusion	Fidelity
20 to 40 years	Intimacy vs. Isolation	Love
40 to 65 years	Generativity vs. Stagnation	Care
65 and older	Integrity vs. Despair	Wisdom

across the lifespan. It provides the age ranges at which differing crises must be resolved successfully or the crises will continue to be issues from the remainder of the person's life. Table 14 includes a breakdown of Erikson's stages.

To begin, newborns need to be cared for. They need to eat and be changed in predictable ways, while enjoying considerable time being held and talked to. This will help them build a basic trust of the world. From this they will develop hope for the future.

During the second stage (1–3 years), children need to be encouraged to explore their surroundings to build autonomy. If they are unsuccessful, they develop a sense of shame. The successful completion of this stage creates a defined will in the person. In the next stage (3–6 years), they need to internalize initiative and some control in their lives. With success, they will develop a sense of purpose. Preschool can contribute greatly to this issue.

Children need to have success in school activities to develop industriousness. To that end, schools are key in providing opportunities for learned skills and productivity. During the next stage (ages 12–20), students need to develop a sense of self and personal identity. If successful, they avoid a being confused about their role while developing fidelity. In the last stage appropriate for this book, children need to develop loving relationships with people to have a sense of intimacy. Not successfully completing this crisis leaves the person feeling isolated. It is easy to see the importance of successfully resolving each crisis to the psychosocial development of the person. Add endogenous characteristics and experiences often associated with students with gifts and talents, and one can see that their lives tend to be more complicated than the average person.

In concert with the strong foundation guided by the work of Erik Erikson, we should be able to help gifted children develop into well-adjusted adults, virtually free from suicidal behavior. Of course we cannot prevent the correlates of suicide outside of the development of the individual gifted child. For example, a family member of a gifted child could complete suicide. These are examples that cannot be affected by developmental parenting. In the fourth edition of my recent book entitled *On the Social and Emotional Lives of Gifted Students* (Cross, 2011), I included ideas for effective parenting, teaching, and guidance of students with gifts and talents. Some of the ideas are used below.

All gifted students should participate from time to time in counseling. Most of the counseling will be educative—teaching prosocial skills, communication skills, how to deal with frustration and stress, and how to wait on other students to catch up. Students would learn about what it means to be a gifted student and how hard work and practice are required to develop their potentials into specific talent domains. In secondary school, they will need considerable college and career counseling. Between the two, they will benefit from having opportunities to discuss friendships and other important relationships. This connection with a well-trained counselor or psychologist will ease the struggle of growing up gifted in our anti-intellectual culture. More serious problems can be identified early and dealt with before they become too serious.

Students with gifts and talents must spend some time together. The amount of time that is ideal is unclear, but time together helps with the feelings of being different that can be troubling during secondary school. I suggest that time in summer residential programs is especially helpful in developing a positive self-concept and possible friendships.

If teachers, counselors, and parents work together on the prevention of suicidal behavior of students with gifts and talents, the odds improve dramatically. Others such as administrators, psychologists, and psychiatrists are available should the more proactive measures taken give way to bad experiences, changes in brain physiology, suicidal correlates, or traumatic events that can accumulate to move a person onto my Spiral Model of the Suicidal Mind of Gifted Children and Adolescents. Should that occur, all of the adults and fellow students should be prepared to play their respective roles to help the student in distress. With sufficient training, we can create a formidable team to prevent suicidal behavior and even heal the suicidal mind of gifted children and adolescents.

KEY POINTS FOR CHAPTER 9

❖ Due to their endogenous characteristics, gifted students encounter challenges to norms early, and oftentimes find themselves in complex social situations.

❖ Gifted students often develop social coping behaviors to protect themselves from mixed messages or anti-intellectual environments.

❖ Some social coping strategies, such as underachievement or going underground, can have negative impacts on their academic success.

❖ During adolescence, fitting in and standing out are often desired at the same time.

❖ The most pervasive threat to mental health of gifted students in school is the mismatch between the school's curriculum and the students' academic needs. As a result, many gifted students operate at less than 50% of their capacity, causing frustration and other problems.

- ❖ Erik Erikson's (1963) Theory of Psychosocial Development provides the age ranges at which differing crises must be resolved successfully or the crises will continue to be issues for the remainder of the person's life.

- ❖ Preschools can contribute greatly to development of the sense of purpose in 3–6 year-olds by helping them to successfully internalize initiative and some control in their lives.

- ❖ Schools play a key role in providing opportunities for learned skills and productivity, and can offer possibilities for success in school activities to develop industriousness.

- ❖ Although we cannot prevent the correlates of suicide outside of the development of the individual gifted child, we can provide helpful ideas and guidelines for effective parenting and teaching of gifted students.

- ❖ All gifted students should participate in counseling, where they can learn about what it means to be gifted, discuss friendships and other important relationships, and receive college and career advice. Counseling will also provide a chance to identify and work through more serious problems at an early stage.

- ❖ When teachers, counselors, and parents work together on the prevention of suicidal behavior of students with gifts and talents, the odds improve dramatically.

Resources

National Resources

National Suicide Prevention Lifeline

This is a 24-hour, toll-free, confidential suicide prevention lifeline and online chat site for people in crisis. Calls are routed to the nearest crisis center in the national network of more than 150 crisis centers. The lifeline provides counseling and mental health referrals.

Hotline: 800-273-8255
Website: http://www.suicidepreventionlifeline.org
Facebook: http://www.facebook.com/800273TALK
Twitter: @800273TALK
YouTube: http://www.youtube.com/user/800273TALK
Online chat: http://suicidepreventionlifeline.org/GetHelp/ LifelineChat.aspx
You Matter Website: http://www.youmatter. suicidepreventionlifeline.org

Kristin Brooks Hope Center

This is a not-for-profit organization that focuses on suicide prevention, awareness, and education. It provides help and hope through crisis hotlines, online crisis chat, and college campus awareness events.

Address: 1250 24th Street NW, Suite 300, Washington, DC 20037
Website: http://hopeline.com
Hotline 1: 800-442-HOPE
Hotline 2: 800-784-2433 or 800-SUICIDA (Spanish)

Teen to teen peer counseling hotline: 877-968-8454 or
877-YOUTHLINE
Online Crisis Network: http://www.IMAlive.org
Online chat crisis support: https://www.imalive.org/chat.
php

JED FOUNDATION

A national organization that works to prevent suicide and
promote emotional health among college and university students,
JED Foundation also supports a student program, "Half of Us."
This is a national campaign to raise awareness about mental health
issues on campus and to connect students to resources to get help.
The organization also has partnered with MTV to produce fea-
tures in which artists discuss their own struggles with mental
health issues.

Address: 1140 Broadway, Ste. 803, New York, NY 10001
Phone: 212-647-7544
Fax: 212-647-7542
Website: http://www.jedfoundation.org/students or http://
www.halfofus.com

THE TREVOR PROJECT

This resource is targeted at LGBTQ youth to provide crisis intervention, a digital community, and advocacy programs.
The organization also sponsors several other resources for youth,
including Ask Trevor, an online question and answer resource for
youths looking for information and guidance on sexual orientation
and gender identity; TrevorChat, a confidential, secure, and free
online messaging service that gives live help to students not at risk
for suicide; and TrevorSpace, an online social networking community for LGBTQ youths (ages 13–24) and their friends/allies.

Address: 8704 Santa Monica Blvd., Ste. 200, West
Hollywood, CA 90069
Hotline: 866-488-7386
Los Angeles Office Phone: 310-271-8845

New York Office Phone: 212-695-8650
Fax: 310-271-8846
Website: http://www.thetrevorproject.org
Ask Trevor Website: http://www.thetrevorproject.org/
    deartrevor
TrevorChat Website: http://www.thetrevorproject.org/
    Programs
TrevorSpace Website: http://trevorspace.org
Facebook: http://www.facebook.com/TheTrevorProject
Twitter: @trevorproject
YouTube: http://www.youtube.com/thetrevorproject

STATE/LOCAL RESOURCES

ALABAMA

Crisis Center
Address: 3600 8th Avenue South, Suite 501, Birmingham,
    AL, 35222
Hotline: 800-273-8255
Phone: 205-323-7777
Fax: 205-328-6225
Website: http://www.crisiscenterbham.com

ALASKA

Careline Crisis Intervention
Address: 726 26th Avenue, Suite 1, Fairbanks, AK 99701
Hotline 1: 877-266-4357
Hotline 2: 800-273-8255
Phone: 800-273-8255
Fax: 457-2442
Website: http://www.carelinealaska.com
Blog: http://www.carelinealaska.com/blog

ARIZONA

EMPACT Suicide Prevention Center
Address: 618 S. Madison Dr., Tempe, AZ 85281
Hotline: 866-205-5229
Phone: 480-784-1514
Website: http://www.empact-spc.com

ARKANSAS

Arkansas Crisis Center
Address: 14 E. Emma, Suite 213, Springdale, AR 72764
Hotline: 888-CRISIS2
Phone: 479-365-2140
Website: http://www.arcrisis.org

CALIFORNIA

WellSpace Health
Address: The Effort Residential Treatment Center, 1550
   Juliesse Ave, Sacramento, CA 95815
Hotline 1: 916-368-3111
Hotline 2: 800-273-8255
Phone: 916-737-5555
Website: http://www.wellspacehealth.org/index.htm
Facebook: https://www.facebook.com/WellSpaceHealth
Twitter: https://twitter.com/wellspacehealth

San Francisco Suicide Prevention
Address: P.O. Box 191350, San Francisco, CA, 94119-1350
Hotline: 415-781-0500
Phone: 415-984-1900
Fax: 415-227-0247
Website: http://www.sfsuicide.org
Facebook: https://www.facebook.com/sfsuicideprevention
Twitter: https://twitter.com/SFSuicide

COLORADO

Metro Crisis Services, Inc.
Address: P.O. Box 460695, Denver, CO 80246
Hotline: 888-885-1222
Website: http://www.metrocrisisservices.org

CONNECTICUT

Department of Mental Health & Addiction Services
Address: 410 Capitol Avenue, PO Box 341431, Hartford, CT 06134
Hotline: 800-446-7348
Phone: 860-418-7000
Website: http://www.dmhas.state.ct.us/crmhc/homepage. htm

DELAWARE

ContactLifeline
Hotline: 800-262-9800
Website: http://www.contactlifeline.org

In New Castle County
Address: PO Box 9525, Wilmington, DE 19809
Hotline: 302-761-9100
Hotline TDD: 302-761-9700
Fax: 302-761-4280

DISTRICT OF COLUMBIA

DC Department of Mental Health
Address: 64 New York Avenue NE, 3rd Floor, Washington, DC 20002
Hotline: 800-273-8255
Phone: 202-673-7440
Fax: 202-673-3433
Website: http://www.IAmTheDifferenceDC.org

In Kent and Sussex Counties
Address: PO Box 61, Milford, DE 19963
Phone: 302-422-1154
Fax: 302-422-2078

FLORIDA

Heart of Florida United Way
Address: Dr. Nelson Ying Center, 1940 Traylor Boulevard, Orlando, FL 32804 (other locations available across the state)
Hotline: 2-1-1
Phone: 407-835-0900
Fax: 407-835-1959

GEORGIA

Behavioral Health Link
Hotline: 800-715-4225
Phone: 404-420-3202
Website: http://www.behavioralhealthlink.com/

HAWAII

ACCESS Line
Address: 1250 Punchbowl Street, Room #256 Honolulu, Hawaii 96813
Hotline: 800-753-6879
Hotline (Oahu Island): 832-3100
Phone: 808-586-4686
Fax: 808-586-4745
Website: http://www.amhd.org/default.asp

ILLINOIS

Community Counseling Centers of Chicago
Address: 4740 N. Clark St., Chicago, IL 60640
Phone: 773-769-0205
Website: http://www.c4chicago.org

Mental Health Centers of Central Illinois
Address: 710 N. Eighth Street, Springfield, Illinois
 62702-6395
Hotline: 800-273-8255
Hotline TDD: 217-588-7805
Phone: 217-525-1064
Fax: 217-525-9047
Website: https://www.mhcci.org

INDIANA

Mental Health American in Greater Indianapolis
Address: 301 East 38th Street, Indianapolis, IN 46205
Hotline: 317-251-7575 or text CSIS to 839863
Phone: 317-251-0005
Fax: 317-254-2800
Website: http://www.mhaindy.net

IOWA

The Crisis Center of Johnson County
Address: 1121 Gilbert Court, Iowa City IA 52240-4528
Hotline: 319-351-0140
Phone: 319-351-2726
Fax: 319-351-4671
Website: http://jccrisiscenter.org

KANSAS

Headquarters Counseling Center
Address: PO Box 999, Lawrence, KS 66044
Hotline: 785-841-2345
Website: http://www.headquarterscounselingcenter.org

KENTUCKY

Crisis and Information Center, Seven Counties Service
Address: 101 West Muhammad Ali Boulevard, Louisville, KY 40202
Hotline 1: 502-589-4313
Hotline 2: 800-221-0446
Phone: 502-589-1100
Fax: 502-589-8614
Website: http://www.sevencounties.org

LOUISIANA

Baton Rouge Crisis Intervention Center
Address: 4837 Revere Avenue, Baton Rouge, LA 70808
Hotline 1: 2-1-1
Hotline 2: 225-924-3900
Hotline 3: 800-437-0303
Phone: 225-924-1431
Website: http://www.brcic.org
Facebook: https://www.facebook.com/brcrisisinterventioncenter
YouTube: http://www.youtube.com/watch?v=Rt_uivFxSIU

MAINE

Crisis and Counseling
Address: 10 Caldwell Road, August, ME 04330
Hotline: 888-568-1112
Phone: 207-626-3448
Fax: 207-621-6228
Website: http://www.crisisandcounseling.org

MARYLAND

Baltimore Crisis Response
Address: 2041 East Fayette Street, Baltimore, MD 21231
Hotline: 410-433-5175
Hotline TDD: 410-433-7050
Phone: 410-433-5255
Fax: 410-433-6795
Website: http://www.bcresponse.org

Frederick County Hotline
Address: 226 South Jefferson Street, Frederick, MD 21701
Hotline: 301-662-2255
Phone: 301-663-0011
Fax: 301-695-4747
Website: http://www.fcmha.org

MASSACHUSETTS

The Samaritans of Boston
Address: 41 West St., 4th Floor, Boston, MA 02111
Hotline 1: 877-870-4673
Hotline 2: 800-252-8336
Hotline 3: 617-247-0220
Hotline 4: 508-875-4500
Website: http://samaritanshope.org

MICHIGAN

Neighborhood Service Organization
Address: 220 Bagley, Suite 1200, Detroit, MI 48226
Hotline: 800-241-4949
Phone: 313-961-4890
Fax: 313-961-5120
Website: http://www.nso-mi.org/
Facebook: https://www.facebook.com/nso.michigan
Twitter: https://twitter.com/nsomichigan
YouTube: http://www.youtube.com/user/NSOMichigan

MINNESOTA

Crisis Connection
Address: 1550 East 78th St., Richfield, MN 55423
Hotline 1: 612-379-6363
Hotline 2: 866-379-6363
Phone: 612-852-2200
Website: http://www.hsicrisis.org

MISSISSIPPI

CONTACT Helpline
Address: PO Box 1304, Columbus, MS 39703
Hotline: 800-377-1643
Phone: 662-327-2968
Fax: 662-244-3454
Website: http://www.contacthelplinegtrms.org
Facebook: https://www.facebook.com/Contacthelplinegtrms
Twitter: https://twitter.com/contactgtr

MISSOURI

Life Crisis Services
Address: 2650 Olive St., St. Louis, MO 63103
Hotline 1: 314-647-4357
Hotline 2: 800-273-8255
Phone: 314-371-6500
Website: http://www.providentstl.org

MONTANA

The Help Center
Address: 421 E. Peach Street, Bozeman, MT 59715
Hotline: 406-586-3333
Website: http://www.bozemanhelpcenter.org

NEBRASKA

Boys Town National Hotline
Address: 14100 Crawford Street, Boys Town, NE 68010
Hotline: 800-448-3000
Phone: 402-498-1300
Website: http://www.boystown.org
Facebook: https://www.facebook.com/BoysTownMission
Twitter: https://twitter.com/BoysTownMission

NEVADA

Crisis Call Center
Address: PO Box 8016, Reno, NV 89507
Hotline: 800-273-8255
Phone: 775-784-8085
Fax: 775-784-8083
Website: http://www.crisiscallcenter.org

NEW HAMPSHIRE

Headrest
Address: 14 Church Street, Lebanon, NH 03766
Hotline: 603-448-4400
Phone: 603-448-4872 (Ext: 110)
Fax: 603-448-1829
Website: http://www.headrest.org

NEW JERSEY

CONTACT of Burlington County
Address: PO Box 333, Moorestown, NJ 08057
Hotline 1: 856-234-8888
Hotline 2: 866-234-5006
Phone: 856-234-5484
Website: http://www.contactburlco.org

NEW MEXICO

Agora Crisis Center
Address: 1820 Sigma Chi Rd., Albuquerque, NM 87131
Hotline: 866-HELP-1-NM
Phone: 505-277-3013
Website: http://www.unm.edu/~agora

NEW YORK

Covenant House
Address: 460 West 41st Street, New York, NY 10036
Hotline: 800-999-9999
Phone: 800-388-3888
Website: http://www.covenanthouse.org
Facebook: https://www.facebook.com/CovenantHouse
Twitter: https://twitter.com/CovenantHouse
YouTube: http://www.youtube.com/user/CovenantHouse

Long Island Crisis Center
Address: 2740 Martin Avenue, Bellmore, NY 11710
Hotline: 516-679-1111
Phone: 516-826-0244
Website: http://www.longislandcrisiscenter.org
Facebook: https://www.facebook.com/longisland.crisiscenter
Twitter: https://twitter.com/LICrisisCenter

NORTH CAROLINA

REAL Crisis Intervention
Address: 1011 Anderson St., Greenville, NC 27858
Hotline: 252-758-4357
Website: http://realcrisis.org
Facebook: https://www.facebook.com/realcrisis
YouTube: http://www.youtube.com/
    watch?v=WNO6TYqLP9A

NORTH DAKOTA

FirstLink Hotline
Address: 4357 13th Ave. S, Ste. 107L, Fargo, ND 58103
Hotline 1: 2-1-1
Hotline 2: 701-235-7335
Phone 1: 701-293-6462
Phone 2: 888-293-6462
Fax: 701-235-2476
Website: http://www.myfirstlink.org/211.shtml
Facebook: https://www.facebook.com/myfirstlink
Twitter: https://twitter.com/myfirstlink_org
YouTube: http://www.youtube.com/user/
myfirstlink?feature=results_main

OHIO

Talbert House
Address: 2600 Victory Parkway, Cincinnati , Ohio
45206-1711
Hotline: 513-281-2273
Phone: 513-751-7747
Fax: 513-751-8107
Website: http://www.talberthouse.org/index.html

North Central Mental Health Services
Address: 1301 North High Street, Columbus, OH 43201
Hotline: 614-221-5445
Phone: 614-299-6600
Website: http://www.ncmhs.org

OKLAHOMA

Heartline
Address: Central Office, 650 S. Peoria Avenue, Tulsa, OK
74120
Hotline: 918-744-4800

Phone: 918-587-9471
Website: http://www.fcsok.org/
Facebook: https://www.facebook.com/fcsok
Twitter: https://twitter.com/FCSTulsa
YouTube: http://www.youtube.com/user/
FamilyandChildrensOK

OREGON

Oregon Partnership-Lines for Life
Address: 5100 SW Macadam Avenue, Suite 400, Portland,
OR 97239
Hotline: 800-273-8255
Phone 1: 503-244-5211
Phone 2: 800-282-7035
Fax: 503-244-5506
Website: http://www.linesforlife.org

PENNSYLVANIA

Re:Solve Crisis Network
Address: 333 North Braddock Avenue, Pittsburgh, PA
15208
Hotline: 888-796-8226
Website: http://upmc.com/Services/behavioral-health/
Pages/resolve-crisis-network.aspx
Facebook: https://www.facebook.com/upmc?ref=nf
YouTube: http://www.youtube.com/upmc

RHODE ISLAND

Gateway/Community Counseling Center
Address: 249 Roosevelt Avenue, Suite 205, Pawtucket, RI
02860
Hotline 1: 401-723-1915
Hotline 2: 401-553-1031
Phone: 401-724-8400
Website: http://www.gatewayhealth.org

SOUTH CAROLINA

United Way Association of South Carolina
Address: 2711 Middleburg Drive, Suite 305, Columbia, SC 29204
Hotline 1: 2-1-1
Hotline 2: 866-892-9211
Phone: 803-929-1000
Fax: 866-488-6462
Website: http://www.tuw.org/211.asp

SOUTH DAKOTA

HELP!Line Center
Address: 1000 N. West Ave, Suite 310, Sioux Falls, SD 57104
Hotline 1: 2-1-1
Hotline 2: 605-339-4357
Website: http://www.helplinecenter.org
Facebook: https://www.facebook.com/HelplineCenter
Twitter: https://twitter.com/HelplineCenter

TENNESSEE

The Crisis Center of Family & Children's Service
Address: 201 23rd Avenue North, Nashville, TN 37203
Hotline: 615-244-7444
Phone: 615-320-0591
Fax: 615-321-3906
Website: http://www.fcsnashville.org

TEXAS

CONTACT Crisis Line
Address: PO Box 800742, Dallas, TX 75830
Hotline: 972-233-2233
Phone: 972-233-0866
Fax: 972-233-2427

Website: http://contactcrisisline.org
Facebook: https://www.facebook.com/
 CONTACTCrisisLine
Twitter: https://twitter.com/contact_crisis

Crisis Intervention of Houston, Inc.
Address: 3701 Kirby Drive, Suite 540, Houston, TX 77098
Hotline: 713-HOTLINE
Phone: 713-533-4500
Website: http://www.crisishotline.org
Facebook: https://www.facebook.com/
 CrisisInterventionofHouston
Twitter: https://twitter.com/Crisis_Hotline

UTAH

UNI CrisisLine
Address: University Neuropsychiatric Institute, 501 Chipeta
 Way, Salt Lake City, UT 84108
Hotline: 801-587-3000
Phone: 801-583-2500
Website: http://healthcare.utah.edu/uni/crisisline

VERMONT

Vermont 2-1-1
Address: PO Box 111, Essex Junction, VT 05453
Hotline 1: 2-1-1
Hotline 2: 866-652-4636
Fax: 802-861-2544
Website: http://www.vermont211.org
Facebook: https://www.facebook.com/Vermont211?sk=info
YouTube: http://www.youtube.com/211vermont

VIRGINIA

CrisisLink
Address: 2503 D. N. Harrison St., #114, Arlington, VA
22204
Hotline: 703-527-4077
Hotline TDD: 7-1-1
Phone: 703-527-6603
Website: http://www.crisislink.org
Facebook: https://www.facebook.com/crisislink

WASHINGTON

Crisis Clinic
Address: 9725 3rd Avenue NE, Suite 300, Seattle, WA
98115
Hotline: 866-427-4747
Phone: 206-461-3210
Fax: 206-461-8368
Website: http://www.crisisclinic.org
Facebook: https://www.facebook.com/
CrisisClinicKingCounty
Twitter: https://twitter.com/CrisisClinic

WEST VIRGINIA

Valley HealthCare System
Address: 301 Scott Avenue, Morgantown, WV 26508
Hotline: 800-232-0020
Phone: 304-296-1731
Fax: 304-225-2288
Website: http://www.valleyhealthcare.org

WISCONSIN

Crisis Center of Family Services
Address: Family Services of Northeast Wisconsin, Inc., 300
    Crooks St., Green Bay, WI 54303
Hotline: 920 436-8888
Phone: 920-436-6800
Fax: 920-432-5966
Website: http://www.familyservicesnew.org
Facebook: https://www.facebook.com/familyservicesnew

WYOMING

Wyoming Behavioral Institute
Address: 2521 E. 15th St., Casper, WY 82609
Hotline: 800-457-9312
Phone: 307-237-7444
Fax: 307-472-2297
Website: http://www.wbihelp.com

Canadian Resources

Alberta

Doctor Margaret Savage Crisis Centre
Address: Box 419, Cold Lake AB T9M 1P1
Hotline: 866-594-0533
Phone: 780-594-5095
Fax: 780-594-7304
Website: http://www.dmscc.ca

British Columbia

The Crisis Intervention and Suicide Prevention Centre of British Columbia
Address: 763 East Broadway, Vancouver, BC V5T 1X8
Hotline: 800-784-2433
Phone: 604-872-1811
Fax: 604-879-6216
Website: http://www.crisiscentre.bc.ca

Manitoba

The Manitoba Suicide Line
Address: C/O Unit 1, 217 10th St., Brandon, MB Canada
Hotline: 877-435-7170
Phone: 204-571-4182
Fax: 204-571-4184
Website: http://www.reasontolive.ca
Facebook: https://www.facebook.com/pages/Reason-To-Live-Manitoba-Suicide-Line/149395961783773

New Brunswick

New Brunswick Suicide Prevention Resource Center
Address: 403 Regent St. Suite 202, Fredericton, NB E3B 3X6
Hotline: 800-667-5005
Phone: 506-455-5231

Fax: 506-459-3878
Website: http://nb.cmha.ca

NEWFOUNDLAND AND LABRADOR

Mental Health Crisis Centre
Address: 47 Street Clare Avenue, St. John's, NF A1C 2J9
Hotline: 888-737-4668
Website: http://www.suicideprevention.ca

NOVA SCOTIA

Mental Health Mobile Crisis Team
Address: PO Box 1004, Dartmouth, NS B2Y 3Z6
Hotline: 902-429-8167
Website: http://www.suicideprevention.ca

ONTARIO

Distress Center Ontario (multiple locations)
Hotline: 800-465-4442
Website: http://www.dcontario.org/centres.html

PRINCE EDWARD ISLAND

Island Helpline
Address: PO Box 1033, Fredericton, PE E3B 5C2
Hotline: 800-218-2885
Website: http://www.suicideprevention.ca/in-crisis-now/
find-a-crisis-centre-now/crisis-centres/crisis-pei

QUÉBEC

Centre de Prévention du Suicide de Québec
Address: 8180 Boulevard Pierre-Bertrand Nord, Québec
(Québec), Canada, G2K 1W1
Hotline: 866-277-3553
Phone: 418-683-0933

Fax: 418-683-5956
Website: http://www.cpsquebec.ca

SASKATCHEWAN

North East Crisis Intervention Centre
Address: 103 McKendry Avenue East, Melfort, SK S0E
1A0
Hotline: 800-611-6349
Phone: 306-752-9464

REFERENCES

American Association of Suicidology. (n.d.). *Know the warning signs.* Retrieved from http://www.suicidology.org/stats-and-tools/suicide-warning-signs

Baker, J. A. (1995). Depression and suicidal ideation among academically talented adolescents. *Gifted Child Quarterly, 39,* 218–223.

Cassady, J. C., & Cross, T. L. (2006). A factorial representation of suicidal ideation among academically gifted adolescents. *Journal for the Education of the Gifted, 29,* 290–304.

Centers for Disease Control and Prevention. (2013). *Injury prevention & control: Suicide prevention.* Retrieved from http://www.cdc.gov/injury/wisqars/index.html

Coleman, L. (1985). *Schooling the gifted.* Menlo Park, CA: Addison-Wesley.

Coleman, L. (2011). Lived experience, mixed messages, and stigma. In T. L. Cross & J. R. Cross (Eds.). Handbook for counselors serving students with gifts and talents (pp. 371–392). Waco, TX: Prufrock Press.

Coleman, L. J., & Cross, T. L. (1988). Is being gifted a social handicap? *Journal for the Education of the Gifted, 11,* 41–56.

Coleman, L. J., & Cross, T. L. (2000). Social-emotional development and the personal experience of giftedness. In K. A. Heller, F. J. Mönks, R. J. Sternberg, & R. F. Subotnik (Eds.), *International handbook of giftedness and talent* (pp. 203–212). Oxford: Elsevier.

Cramond, B., & Martin, C. E. (1987). Inservice and preservice teachers' attitudes toward the academically brilliant. *Gifted Child Quarterly, 31,* 15–19.

Cross, T. L. (1996a, January). Examining claims about gifted children and suicide. *Gifted Child Today, 19*(1), 46–48.

Cross, T. L. (1996b, May/June). Social and emotional needs of gifted students: Psychological autopsy provides insight into gifted adolescent suicide. *Gifted Child Today, 19*(3), 22–50.

Cross, T. L. (2008). Suicide. In J. A. Plucker & C. M. Callahan (Eds.), *Critical issues and practices in gifted education: What the research says* (1st ed., pp. 629–639). Waco, TX: Prufrock Press.

Cross, T. L. (2011). *On the social and emotional lives of gifted children* (4th ed.). Waco, TX: Prufrock Press.

Cross, T. L., Cassady, J. C., & Miller, T. (2006). Suicidal ideation and psychological type in gifted adolescents. *Gifted Child Quarterly, 19*, 46–48.

Cross, T. L., Coleman, L. J., & Stewart, R. A. (1993). The school-based social cognition of gifted adolescents: An exploration of the stigma of giftedness paradigm. *Roeper Review, 16*, 37 40.

Cross, T. L., Coleman, L. J., & Terhaar-Yonkers, M. (1991). The social cognition of gifted adolescents in schools: Managing the stigma of giftedness. *Journal for the Education of the Gifted, 15*, 44–55.

Cross, T. L., Cook, R. S., & Dixon, D. N. (1996). Psychological autopsies of three academically talented adolescents who committed suicide. *Journal of Secondary Gifted Education, 7*, 403–409.

Cross, T. L., Cross, J. R., & Gong, X. (2009). *The structure of suicidal ideation of honors college students.* Unpublished manuscript.

Cross, T. L., Gust-Brey, K., & Ball, B. (2002). A psychological autopsy of the suicide of an academically gifted student: Researchers' and parents' perspectives. *Gifted Child Quarterly, 46*, 247–264.

Cross, T. L., Stewart, R. A., & Coleman, L. J. (2003). Phenomenology and its implications for gifted studies research: Investigating the *Lebenswelt* of academically gifted students attending an elementary magnet school. *Journal for the Education of the Gifted, 26*, 201–220.

Cross, T. L., & Swiatek, M. A. (2009). Social coping among academically gifted students in a residential setting: A longitudinal study. *Gifted Child Quarterly, 53,* 25–33.

Dabrowski, K. (1964). *Positive disintegration.* Boston, MA: Little, Brown.

Dabrowski, K. (1972). *Psychoneurosis is not an illness.* London, England: Gryf.

Delisle, J. (1986). Death with honors: Suicide among gifted adolescents. *Journal of Counseling and Development, 64,* 558–560.

Delisle, J. R. (1990). The gifted adolescent at risk: Strategies and resources for suicide prevention among gifted youth. *Journal of Education of the Gifted, 13,* 212–228.

DeLisle, M. M., & Holden, R. R. (2009). Differentiating between depression, hopelessness, and psychache in university undergraduates. *Measurement and Evaluation in Counseling and Development, 42,* 46–63.

Dixon, D. N., Cross, T. L., Cook, R., & Scheckel, J. (1995). Gifted-adolescent suicide: Database vs. speculation. *Research Briefs, 10*(1), 45–50.

Durkheim, E. (1951). *Suicide.* Glencoe, IL: The Free Press.

Eckert, T. L., Miller, D.N., DuPaul, G. J., & Riley-Tillman, T. C. (2003). Adolescent suicide prevention: School psychologists' acceptability of school-based programs. *School Psychology Review, 32,* 57–76

Erikson, E. H. (1963). *Childhood and society* (2nd ed.). New York, NY: Norton.

Falk, G. (2001). *Stigma: How we treat outsiders.* Amherst, NY: Prometheus Books

Fleith, D. S. (1998). Suicide among talented youngsters: A sociocultural perspective. *Gifted Education International, 13,* 113–120.

Fleith, D. D. (2001). Suicide among gifted adolescents: How to prevent it. *National Research Center for the Gifted and Talented Newsletter,* Spring. Retrieved from http://www.gifted.uconn.edu/nrcgt/newsletter/spring01/sprng012.html

Goffman, E. (1963). *Stigma: Notes on the management of spoiled identity.* New York, NY: The Free Press.

Gould, M. A., Greenberg, T., Velting, D. M., & Shaffer, D. (2003). Youth suicide risk and preventive interventions: A review of the past 10 years. *Journal of the American Academy of Child and Adolescent Psychiatry, 42,* 386–405.

Howley, C., Howley, A., & Pendarvis, E. (1995). *Out of our minds: Anti-intellectualism and talent development for American schooling.* New York, NY: Teachers College Press.

Hoyert, D. L., & Xu, J. Q. (2012). Deaths: Preliminary data for 2011. *National Vital Statistics Reports, 61*(6). Hyattsville, MD: National Center for Health Statistics.

Husserl, E. (1970). *The crisis of European sciences and transcendental phenomenology: An introduction to phenomenology* (D. Carr, Trans.). Evanston, IL: Northwestern University Press.

Kaiser, C. F., & Berndt, D. J. (1985). Predictors of loneliness in the gifted adolescent. *Gifted Child Quarterly, 29,* 74–77.

King, C. (1997). Suicidal behavior in adolescence. In R. Maris, M. Silverman, & S. Canetto (Eds.), *Review of suicidology* (pp. 61–95). New York, NY: Guilford.

Ludwig, A. (1995). *The price of greatness.* New York, NY: Guilford.

North Carolina State Center for Health Statistics. (2002). *BRFSS survey results 2001 for nationwide firearms.* Retrieved from http://www.schs.state.nc.us/SCHS/brfss/2001/us/firearm3.html

No Child Left Behind Act, 20 U.S.C. §6301 (2001).

Pelkonen, M., & Marttunen, M. (2003). Child and adolescent suicide: Epidemiology, risk factors, and approaches to prevention. *Pediatric Drugs, 5,* 243–265.

Reynolds, C. R. (1987). Raising intelligence: Clever Hans, Candides, and the miracle in Milwaukee. *Journal of School Psychology, 25,* 309–312.

Rudd, M. D., Berman, A. L., Joiner, T. E., Nock, M. K., Silverman, M. M., Mandrusiak, M., & White, T. (2006). Warning signs for suicide: Theory, research, and clinical applications. *Suicide*

& Life-Threatening Behavior, 36, 255–262. doi:10.1521/suli.2006.36.3.255

Sak, U. (2004). A synthesis of research on psychological types of gifted adolescents. *Journal of Secondary Gifted Education, 15,* 70–79.

Schneidman, E. (1981). Suicide thoughts and reflections. *Suicide and Life-Threatening Behavior, 11,* 198–231.

Schneidman, E. S. (1993). *Suicide as psychache: A clinical approach to self-destructive behavior.* Northvale, NJ: Jason Aronson.

Schneidman, E. S. (1998). *The suicidal mind.* Oxford, England: Oxford University Press.

Stillion, J. M., & McDowell, E. E. (1996). *Suicide across the life span.* Washington, DC: Taylor & Francis.

Stillion, J. M., McDowell, E., & May, J. (1984). Developmental trends and sex differences in adolescent attitudes toward suicide. *Death Education, 8,* 81–90.

Street, S., & Kromney, J. D. (1994). Relationship between suicidal behavior and personality types. *Suicide and Life-Threatening Behavior, 24,* 282–292.

Southern, W. T., & Jones, E. D. (1991). (Eds.). *The academic acceleration of gifted children.* New York, NY: Teachers College Press.

Tannenbaum, A. (1983). *Gifted children.* New York, NY: Macmillan.

Turner, J., & Keller, A. (2011). *Leading cause of mortality among college students at 4-year institutions.* Retrieved from https://apha.confex.com/apha/139am/webprogram/Paper241696.html

White, J. (2012). *Preventing youth suicide: A guide for practioners.* Victoria, BC: Ministry of Children and Family Development. Retrieved from http://www.mcf.gov.bc.ca/suicide_prevention/pdf/pys_practitioners_guide.pdf

ABOUT THE
AUTHOR

Dr. Tracy L. Cross holds an endowed chair, Jody and Layton Smith Professor of Psychology and Gifted Education, and is the Executive Director of the Center for Gifted Education at The College of William and Mary. Previously he served Ball State University as the George and Frances Ball Distinguished Professor of Psychology and Gifted Studies, the founder and Executive Director of both the Center for Gifted Studies and Talent Development, and the Institute for Research on the Psychology of the Gifted Students. He has published more than 150 articles, book chapters, and columns; made more than 200 presentations at conferences, and has published six books. He has edited four journals in the field of gifted studies (*Gifted Child Quarterly, Roeper Review, Journal of Secondary Gifted Education, Research Briefs*) and is the current editor of the *Journal for the Education of the Gifted*. He received the Distinguished Scholar Award in 2011 from the National Association for Gifted Children (NAGC), and the Distinguished Service Award from both The Association for the Gifted (TAG) and NAGC. He also received the Early Leader and Early Scholar Awards from NAGC and in 2009 was given the Lifetime Achievement Award from the MENSA Education and Research Foundation. In 2004, he was named the Outstanding Researcher for Ball State University. He serves as the President-Elect of the National Association for Gifted Children.

In addition to an active scholarly agenda, for 9 years he served as the Executive Director of the Indiana Academy for Science, Mathematics and Humanities, a residential high school for intellectually gifted adolescents. He has served as director of two state associations for gifted (Wyoming Association for Gifted Education and Indiana Association for the Gifted). He also served as president of TAG and on the Board and Executive Committee of the NAGC. He will become the President of the National Association for Gifted Children on September 1, 2013.

He lives in Williamsburg, VA, with his wife, Dr. Jennifer Riedl Cross, four children (Ian, Keenan, Colin, Eva) and Bob, the English bulldog.